KT-133-653

TALKING TO YOUR SOLICITOR

Talking to Your Solicitor

Mary Kotsonouris

GILL AND MACMILLAN

Published in Ireland by
Gill and Macmillan Ltd
Goldenbridge
Dublin 8
with associated companies in
Auckland, Budapest, Gaborone, Harare, Hong Kong,
Kampala, Kuala Lumpur, Lagos, London, Madras,
Manzini, Melbourne, Mexico City, Nairobi,
New York, Singapore, Sydney, Tokyo, Windhoek
© Mary Kotsonouris 1992
0 7171 1987 4
Print origination by
Seton Music Graphics Ltd, Bantry, Co. Cork
Printed by Colour Books Ltd, Dublin

A catalogue record is available for this book from the
British Library.

This book is dedicated to all those solicitors who provide a bridge over troubled waters for their clients—and to one in particular.

CONTENTS

INTRODUCTION

My hope is that this book will be of help to those who are concerned about any matter which has legal implications, and are thinking about consulting a solicitor. It is natural that they should like to have a general outline of the law in relation to their interest and to understand the specific way a solicitor could assist them. It would be foolhardy to say that all their questions will be answered or their problems solved, but the book should provide signposts to paths that might be useful to explore. There are aspects of law underlying our individual, domestic and communal lives. For many, they rarely come to the surface, but people confronted with an unfamiliar situation are in a better position to take decisions if they have some knowledge of the principles that govern this hitherto unknown territory.

The book, then, is not a legal handbook, nor does it claim to make an exhaustive trawl of all the possible permutations that must qualify any given answers to questions of law. It is quite true to say that lawyers must have as many arms as an octopus has legs, since they use the phrase, 'on the other hand' so often. The reason is that the answer to any legal question depends on the very precise circumstances of the particular case. The relevant law is sketched in, therefore, with broad lines, so as to give the reader a background against which personal situations can be measured. At the end of the day, whether legal advice is sought or not will depend on how important the matter is to the individual concerned.

The subject matter is drawn both from my experience as a solicitor and from the very different perspective that a judge acquires in hearing people tell their own stories in court. However, even more than I have learned from either career, this book is the product of countless conversations that I have had with all kinds of people since I was first apprenticed to the law, thirty years ago. They wonder about making a will, are upset by confrontations in court: they are saddened by the general unfairness of life, but sustain the hope that decent behaviour will succeed in the long run. Such hope is often invested in the legal process, perhaps wrongly. People forget that the law is also a human institution and they are frequently disappointed when it fails to live up to their expectations.

A solicitor is seen as a bridge between the person who has a problem and the law from which she or he expects a solution. If their encounter ultimately results in frustration or disappointment, then suspicion of the whole system is further deepened: it results in an unjustified cynicism on the basis of one experience. Such a blight on hope is frequently due to a lack of communication. Clients need encouragement to work through their anger, dismay or a sense of misplaced trust, before they can reach a sober decision on what is in their real interest. Solicitors, at home in a world of proofs, precedent and legislation, can wrongly attribute to the client an understanding of what has been explained, simply because the right questions were not asked. They often fail to notice that clients may feel uncomfortable with the advice given because it is contrary to their instinctual behaviour towards other people. If this book helps some clients and solicitors to establish and maintain a more confident cooperation with one another, it will have been worthwhile.

Lastly, I refer to the imaginary solicitor as 'he' throughout. Having practised as a solicitor for fifteen years, I know that a lawyer, whether solicitor or barrister, is as likely to be a woman as a man. Yet it saves a lot of typing if one does not have to offer a choice of gender in every sentence, with the necessary subsequent choice of personal pronouns and adjectives. I have, therefore, followed the legal usage of the masculine form to include the feminine.

I am very grateful to many of the agencies listed at the end of the book, who graciously and enthusiastically gave so much of their time to answer my questions and who sent me their publications. Heartfelt thanks are also expressed to all the friends who told me of their experiences as clients and solicitors.

WHO NEEDS SOLICITORS?

Solicitors, as a class of persons, do not have instant appeal. Think of all those doctor-and-nurse romances: there are not many tender tales of solicitor-and-clerk, or solicitor-and-client encounters in the popular fiction shelves of the local library—although there was a woman who fell in love with the barrister representing her in a court action, and later married him. In fact, lawyers do not figure much as heroes in plays or novels: in cowboy films they tend to wear black hats and turn out to be the villain. The only chance they get to shine from the pages of a book is when they happen to be amateur detectives as well.

Many people who have never knowingly talked to a solicitor in their lives will tell you that they are all dishonest, manipulative or in cahoots with one another. Thoughtful people realise that they are likely to be as mixed a bag as any other group—that there are good solicitors, nervous ones, incompetent ones. Nevertheless there are doubts to be overcome, initially because the immensity and complexity of the law is filtered through them to us. This kind of witch-doctor image makes the laity hesitant and defensive in its approaches, and it naturally leads to a feeling of resentment which will fade only if a relationship of trust and goodwill is established equally on both sides.

The fact that we very often go to a solicitor about a difficult situation means we are already angry or confused. We cannot quite see what they are going to do for us, and there certainly will not be any immediate result from our visit. The doctor writes a prescription or sends you for a hospital examination. The mechanic bends over the stalled engine, pulling at bits of wire, and suddenly the car starts. The Lovelier You emerges under the skilled hands of the hairdresser, while you look on in the mirror. But when you come out of a solicitor's office, you have nothing to show for it, and it is still not clear to you what he is going to do, even if he has done his best to explain.

Sometimes the dilemma is whether or not you need a solicitor. Perhaps you will instruct one, only to realise, several months later, that you did not need him at all. Equally, if you do nothing, you may have reason soon to conclude that it would have been better to be sure than sorry, as you are now. It is not much help to tell you that it really is a matter for yourself. It certainly cannot do any harm to sit down and consider the alternatives.

Apart from wise and loving friends, who else can give us sound advice or take our part in troubled times? There are local Information Centres, the Ombudsman, our elected representatives, local, national or European; there is the Community Care Officer, the health visitor, and if the trouble is a spouse, there are Marriage Guidance Counsellors and the Mediation Service. There is nothing to be lost in thinking about these professionals first, or even approaching one or more to see if they can help. If they are convinced that you should consult a solicitor, they will tell you. It is advice you should certainly take.

Another thing you may find of immense benefit is sitting down and writing out your own case, as it occurred. By writing it out for yourself you can perhaps see another way of resolving whatever is troubling you. Doing this will probably isolate the issues and reveal the importance you place on them, as well as help to highlight the main incidents. Hold on to your own account of everything; later, you may need to add other factors that occur to you. If you do decide to go to a solicitor, bring your sheets of paper with you. Many bright solicitors ask clients to make this kind of preparation anyway, because they have found it helpful to both parties.

Apart from making the decision to consult a solicitor yourself, events may take a course which propels you to act in this way. It might be a letter from another solicitor, saying that your inoffensively parked car has reared up and attacked his client's car, causing thousands of pounds' worth of damage! Unless he receives a letter by return, humbly accepting all blame and undertaking to put all your worldly goods, unreservedly, at the disposal of his client, proceedings will follow in twenty-four hours. It may be that your local authority is slapping Compulsory Purchase Orders on every front garden in your street for some grandiose scheme you know nothing about. Or a letter, deckle-edged and embossed in gold, with about forty partners' names, arrives from California to tell you that you are among an unspecified number of heirs of your late Great Uncle Willie, the former gold prospector, and if you sign the enclosed, their Mr Grappelunger will deal with it all. The last communication will certainly convince you of the need for someone to speak on your behalf, loud and clear, if nothing else does.

Where are you going to find a solicitor? Will he take your case; will he be any good? The second question is the easier one to answer. Most solicitors are sitting in offices for which they are paying rent, rates and repairs, waiting for clients to come along to help them do it. You will find them in the Yellow Pages, or the Incorporated Law Society (whose address is on page 88) will give you the names of those practising in your locality. These days, solicitors also advertise. It will be a great blessing if you can manage to find one near you; it will save a lot of hassle looking up bus timetables or parking your car. If you get to like the first solicitor, you will find it comforting to remember that he is close by.

A personal recommendation is helpful, but it has its pitfalls. The recommended solicitor may not appeal to you, so reserve your judgment and keep your options open until you have met him. It would also be smarter not to mention the friend who made the recommendation until you have decided to go ahead. Indeed, there is no need to mention the friend at all. Perhaps you have a friend who practises as a solicitor, but we are all conscious of the dangers that lurk in a business relationship with friends. You could find it more rewarding to make a friend of your solicitor, than doing things the other way round.

It is probably better to make your own independent enquiries. The firm's name will not convey anything to you, and indeed the partners can have totally different names. You may dread a young whipper-snapper and long for a grave, parental figure. Here is where the Incorporated Law Society comes in handy. You ring them and ask for the names of the principals in Messrs Languid, Leary and Co. and the year in which each of them qualified. Every solicitor has to be a member of the Incorporated Law Society to practise, so do not ask them for an endorsement. The Society would not award anyone a certificate to practise unless it could recommend him.

But it will be delighted with the intelligent interest shown by a member of the public in the important matter of which of their many members she is going to choose to represent her. If you have a list of several firms, you can get all the information about them at the one time.

Now you are ready to make an appointment. Insist on speaking to whomever you have picked, always provided that he is going to be available in the immediate future. Explain that you are thinking of hiring him, but first you wish to speak to him. Tell him briefly about the matter on which you need advice and ask what his consultation fee will be. There is no earthly reason why mentioning money should give rise to awkwardness. You would not buy a piece of meat from the butcher, or a box of nails in the hardware shop, without asking the price. In fact, it will make for greater ease, when you do meet, to have the matter of a fee already out of the way. You will not be anxious about the unknown cost, and the solicitor will have no reason to fear that the friendly atmosphere will freeze if there is a sudden reference to money.

TALKING TO YOUR SOLICITOR

2

You have made an appointment and are off to talk to a solicitor. Save time by bringing any relevant letters, documents and receipts. If you have written out your own account of your case, bring that with you too. You will find it helpful as a reminder of the points that are important. Be sure to be on time, so that you get full value out of the half-hour, or whatever, and that you will have the solicitor's undivided attention. You will also need enough time to sum him up and see whether he is going to suit you or not.

There is no reason to feel diffident or apologetic if you do not know the law. We usually do not apologise to the dentist for our inability to extract our own teeth; we are paying him for his skill. Have a jotter or paper with you to make notes of what the solicitor is saying to you. If he uses terms you do not understand, and does not explain them (as he should), then ask him to do so, and give him a black mark.

However, if the solicitor has taken time to explain a process as best he can, and you still do not understand, then you may have a problem. Ask yourself if you are resisting what he is telling you because you have not yet persuaded yourself that you really want to deal with the matter. You would be much better off having a long talk with yourself first, before making a definite decision to involve other people.

There may be particular things you do not want to tell your solicitor. All right; it may not be necessary. People sometimes blurt out things at consultations, and regret it afterwards. Everyone has privacies they would prefer to guard. As the conversation goes on, you will get a clearer idea of what is relevant. You must not tell your solicitor lies. It is unfair to lie to him and allow him perhaps to make confident assertions on your behalf, in letters or in court, which his opposition can demolish in seconds. Many people expect their solicitor to tell their lies for them, lies that they, themselves, would feel too honest to utter. In any case, it is unforgivable to attempt to make another person a party to your fraud.

These are general guidelines. In most cases, such difficulties do not arise, and clients manage to give a reasonably clear picture of the problem. Any worthwhile and sensitive solicitor can take up whatever slack remains, without blunder or hurt.

What is hurtful to a solicitor is when a client feels it necessary to explain that some confidence is for his ears only. Discretion comes as naturally to a solicitor as breathing. From the day he becomes apprenticed, he solemnly covenants *not* to reveal the secrets of his master's clients. If he were to do so, or discuss his client's business without authority, he would be liable to have his name struck off the register. His business *is* other people's secrets. If you happen to run into your solicitor socially, you have no need to worry that he will be busy recalling confidences or circumstances about which you might feel some embarrassment. He can no more carry around everyone's file in his head, than the assistant in the supermarket can remember when you last bought tea, apart from which, he is out at a party too, and wants to enjoy himself.

Feel free to ask the solicitor about the probable costs of whatever you are contemplating: which costs are recoverable from any other party and which are not. Costs can be estimated, and you certainly should inform yourself about the lowest and the highest figure possible. You may then wish to consider the whole matter again, at your leisure.

You may have a lot of grievances to air, so the solicitor should give you time to get them all off your chest. When you have done so, do not be cross if he reins you back a bit from going over the same ground, in order to concentrate your mind, and his, on hard facts. If it is a matter that may lead to a court case—and it frequently is—be warned that a judge will be far less indulgent in cutting off irrelevancies than any solicitor.

Ask the solicitor all the questions that occur to you, but listen carefully to him if he is explaining the law, or telling you what you will require by way of proof. This is what you are paying for. It is no use interrupting with the account of the enormous damages your neighbour's cousin in Mullingar got for the same thing. There is no comment, helpful or otherwise, the solicitor can make about that. You will break his heart if you imply that you have practically ordered the Securicor vans to stand by to receive the substantial compensation that you know you are going to get. Nothing depresses a solicitor more than impossible expectations raised by stories of sensational awards, when he knows that your case is not comparable.

By now, you will have some idea of your reaction to the solicitor. First impressions are important, so are second, but you might not have that amount of time. It is a sensible idea to pay the solicitor the consultation fee at the end of the first meeting, whether or not another appointment is made. That will give you an opportunity to mull over his advice, and also allows you time to decide on the next step. If you have paid him, he cannot reasonably be aggrieved, even if you do not return. You will not feel that you have committed yourself to a person or to a course, without first taking back control of the situation.

If you do not warm to the solicitor—if you have been patronised, if you think he is a bit too slick—you do not have to stay with him. A great many people feel locked into a relationship with a solicitor, either through laziness or because of the theory that it is better to stay with an unsatisfactory solicitor than take the risk of changing. It is one of those wise saws that is impossible to disprove. If you stay with the solicitor, how will you ever know that things would have been a lot better with someone else?

On the other hand, he might grow on you, but I would not advise that he be given endless chances to do so. The longer you stay, the more dependent on him you are going to become. Remember, too, that it is easier for you to get out of the relationship than for him. Most solicitors have some clients they cannot abide, but usually they feel obliged to offer it up!

I'LL SEE YOU IN COURT

3

So it is definitely going ahead and all attempts at settlement, furtive or otherwise, have come to nothing. You feel in turn elated, depressed, calm and, underneath, sick with anxiety. There is only a little you can do to alleviate any of these symptoms, but you certainly can do something right away to ensure that they do not persist long after the crisis is over. Try not to talk interminably about it to anyone who will listen, even though you cannot stop going over it all in your mind and rehearsing your speech from the dock. The less you tell all and sundry, the less you will need to give a blow-by-blow account of the ordeal later on.

This will help you to put it out of your mind as soon as possible afterwards, which is what you should be aiming for, win or lose. Remember all those people who have held your tolerance level by the very throat, while they regaled you with detail after detail of the case resulting from a damaged mudguard on the road to Doolin in 1973? Or the distant relative who could be relied upon to tell any gathering the story of the large acres the family would have owned if only the land had not been grabbed by unscrupulous persons. You do not want to be like them. You are far too bright to allow a legal dispute to shape the rest of your life, although there are some people who carry on as if eternity is going to be spent in the re-hearing of old court cases. There will be no time to learn the harp or reminisce with loving friends; we shall all be much too busy giving evidence.

If you are very, very lucky, you will need to talk only to your solicitor. Most people will not have one who instinctively knows the appropriate moment for the sly joke or the comforting flash of partisanship, not to mention the odd legal irreverence. If you do, cherish him; he is a pearl beyond price. Otherwise, talk to one friend to whom you will be able to pour out your fears and doubts, or flaunt your confidence beforehand. Yet you will be sure in the knowledge that if you compromise your resolution on the day, by settling for a measly thousand, or leaving the matrimonial court on the arm of the erring spouse for a second honeymoon, your first thought will not be 'I'll hate having to tell so-and-so'.

Your solicitor will go spare if you keep ringing him to ask when or how your case is coming on. Too bad about him, yes—but don't start an unnecessary row with him at this point; there will be plenty of time for that later on. If the paperwork has been completed and the case entered in the Court List for hearing in October, then it is pointless getting him rattled by enquiring in mid-August about its progress. That is a weak ground to choose, if you want to shake him up a bit. Instead, get as positive a date as possible from him nearer the time and think about the questions to which you want answers before the action begins. If a barrister has been instructed, insist on a consultation with him a few days before. Presumably, you will have had one already, when the proceedings were begun. Find out if the solicitor is going to be at the courthouse, or, if he is sending his assistant, where will he be? How will you know him? Where are you to go?

If you have never been in a court, why not pay a leisurely visit a few weeks beforehand? Stroll around the place, no one will pounce on you and ask you what your business is; it is *your* court just as much as it is the Chief Justice's. Then you will not have every unfamiliar thing happening together. Go in and sit there for a while. Unfortunately, you will not hear very much; the acoustics are terrible. You will probably be surprised how low-key it all is, in both senses of the word. It will seem dull and very quiet. There are certain formalities, however, which you must observe. Don't read a newspaper; don't eat your picnic lunch; don't remove more of your clothing than is decent, no matter how warm you find it. One other hint: do not hold a long whispered conversation with someone; no sound rises higher in the general silence than a series of hisses.

What about the barrister? Your solicitor says this is a case for counsel (a sort of collective word for barristers). No doubt he will ask you if you have any preference, and you will murmur something on the lines of 'whatever you are having yourself', as countless clients have done before you. He will tell you that Mr Bleatworthy is excellent on tenants' rights, or Ms Corncrake is the authority on licensing, but does it help? You may also be afraid that your solicitor is giving a hand-out to some youngster who was called to the bar last week. That is a bit unfair; after all, we must presume he wants to win your case, too. What you could do is: when he recommends someone and gives his reasons, ask him whom he would recommend if so-and-so is not available. Then ask him why he would be inclined to choose the first one over the second. This is not to be a clever dick. It is to give you a handle on why a solicitor may think a barrister suitable for a particular case. In the discussion that follows you will get a useful insight into how the presentation of your case in court is assessed.

On the other hand, some people, when asked if they have a preference, will mention the name of a barrister who has figured in several sensational trials in the recent past. If your solicitor noticeably gulps, he is not just being obstructive. Yours is a breach of contract action and you want the best criminal lawyer in the land to act for you. Apart from the cost, it may be twenty years since the great man did a civil case. In any event, all of us cannot have heard of everyone else in the world, and there are lots of very effective barristers whose names we have not noticed at the bottom of a newspaper account of an interesting case. Having your name on everyone's lips is not the only test of excellence in any sphere, as we all know.

Be sure you know where you are to meet your legal team. Do not bring a crowd with you; bring a book and an understanding friend. There will be a lot of waiting about. There is not much you can do about the sick feeling, except to tell yourself, firmly and repeatedly, that you will live through it and come out the other side. This is the time you are most vulnerable to offers of settlement—any offer, any settlement. It is also where a good solicitor becomes a saint. He will keep cool and detached even while the barristers have been talking and teasing out the issues and it invariably puts certain pressure on a solicitor, too.

The most unfortunate thing is that it all happens when the case is about to be, or in some cases, has been, called. It is the moment of crisis; the lawyers have, of course, been fencing around and haggling. Keep a cool head. If you have talked it through beforehand with your solicitor, it will not overwhelm you. However, you have every right to feel appalled if you have been told for months that the very least you can expect is £5,000 and now the same person is urging you to take £450. It is not to be borne. It is time for *you* to start asking the questions.

The question you must *not* ask anyone is 'What would *you* do?' It is not only unfair to put that sort of responsibility on anyone else; it is irrelevant. The answer will depend upon whether the person is timid, fatalistic, far-seeing or a gambler. When a solicitor says that the decision is up to you alone, he is speaking the simple truth. Neither is it fair to think that it is all a put-up job between consenting barristers. Through their encircling chat, your counsel may have glimpsed a weakness in your case that had not been discernible up to that point. It is infinitely better that it is pointed out now, before the other side manages to make a veritable feast of it in court. Nobody can foresee in any detail the way a case will unfold, and that causes lawyers to look keenly at a reasonable offer to settle. But your solicitor and yourself will have discussed this some time before, and agreed on the figure below which no settlement would be made in view of all the time and trouble expended. At least, you have something solid to measure all these last-minute manoeuvrings against. Whatever you decide, make another decision: that there will be no looking back in useless regret, whatever way it turns out. This will give you a more positive outlook in an otherwise wobbly situation.

The actual courtroom scene will not closely resemble the set of your favourite television programme, but it will look enough like it to give you a general idea of the procedure. The props will be the same. You will swear or affirm (to affirm is to make a solemn declaration to tell the truth without having the Bible or Koran in your hand) to tell the truth. By the way, do not listen to anyone who says that your evidence is somehow downgraded when you affirm rather than swear. On the contrary, you have obviously thought about the nature of the oath. The offence of perjury consists of lying to the court when one has given a solemn undertaking not to do so.

Accept beforehand that the other side is going to try and trip you up; that it their job. Your barrister will do the same thing to their witnesses in turn. This is called the adversarial system. It is the only one we have got, although we could change it, presumably, if we all agreed. If you feel it should be changed, then do something about it—but *not* while your case is going on. Therefore, when you are asked a question, answer 'Yes' 'No' or 'I don't know'. If opposing counsel's questions do not admit of any of those answers, then he is in the wrong job.

This is the part of the proceedings where people become a bit bothered. They want to answer the question in their own way. They may not. It is called cross-examination. You are being asked questions on what you have already said in evidence. It is up to your own counsel to bring your version out in direct examination; that is when he takes you through your story. After you have answered 'Yes' or 'No', you may then amplify or qualify your reply, if you wish. On the other hand, you may be of the reasonable opinion that it is not your place to earn the questioner's fee for him. Try not to take it personally, even if some stranger is intent on making you appear a liar in public. It will be over soon, and then your crowd will start peppering your opponent with difficult questions.

You win and your lawyer applies for the costs of the action to be paid to you. As a general rule, such an application will be successful, but costs are at the discretion of the court, which may order that each side is to bear its own, if it is satisfied that this is fairer under all the circumstances. Every single item of expense incurred by the plaintiff is not necessarily recoverable even if awarded costs, and a client should discuss this aspect before proceedings are issued.

Clients of solicitors are often disappointed to find that considerable deductions have to be made out of the compensation awarded to them, either because they have forgotten all about them, or they have not understood the basis on which the court arrived at the final sum. It must be remembered that over the time preceding the action, a solicitor will probably have given undertakings to pay certain debts incurred by his client out of any damages that may eventually be awarded. An obvious example would be a hospital bill following on a motor car accident. You may not be in a position to discharge it, and the hospital agrees to await the outcome of your claim against the other driver. The solicitor has a professional duty to honour any undertaking he has given on your behalf before paying over the balance to you. That is why it is wise to check with him, before the hearing, on the various amounts that have to be paid. Remember, too, that if you have obtained an advance from a bank in the light of your forthcoming action, considerable interest will probably have accumulated by the time the case gets heard. It means that there is a sizeable chunk to come out of what might at first have appeared a substantial sum.

My father, who hated lawyers, used to tell, with great glee, the story of a Limerick labourer who had a serious accident involving a ladder. His solicitor made a successful claim under the Workmen's Compensation Acts and explained, at great length and with circumlocution, the costs and outlay that had to be deducted. He handed the bewildered man the very small residue, and enquired condescendingly if he had any questions. 'Just the one, sir,' said the workman. 'Was it you or me fell off the ladder?'

Another source of possible disappointment can be the attempt to get payment of the amount awarded. You may have to take out an execution order, which the local sheriff will levy against your opponent's goods, or you could register the judgment as a charge on his property, if he has any. It may even be necessary, in the long run, to apply to the District Court for an order that the money be paid by instalments.

All these considerations, while doubtless taken into account, do not seem to prevent many people going to court. They feel the need to tell their grievance aloud to a judge in the presence of their adversary and in a confrontational setting. As long as they are prepared for some of their illusions to be shattered, it is, at least, a better way to try to settle disputes than with sticks and stones!

THE ARM OF THE LAW

4

The majority of the law-abiding public has only intermittent contact with the police and, naturally, tends to be uncertain of the right approach, apart from a vague desire to be helpful. They are hesitant about their own rights or afraid to assert them in case they be seen in a bad light. Those rights, however, have evolved over years and should not be abandoned simply because we have nothing to hide. Eternal vigilance may be the price of not living in a police state.

Innocent persons can find themselves in situations which suddenly turn menacing. Perhaps you become aware that some fellow guests at a party are smoking funny-smelling cigarettes. You are out shopping with a friend who asks you to hold on to a bulging bag and disappears. Or it may be that you are asked to lie about someone else's whereabouts on a certain evening. It is not a great help that you have done nothing wrong; there is a real danger of guilt by association. At these times, one's first loyalty is to oneself, and not to the kind of friends who have no hesitation about embroiling others in their dodgy doings. The prudent course in the above imaginary scenarios is to detach oneself, firmly and quickly.

An arrested person is informed that he does not have to say anything, but if he does, it will be written down and may be given later in evidence. It is not a formula; it is telling you what is going to happen. If you find yourself in just such a position, you are entitled to call a solicitor and have him represent you from that moment. This is one time you do not have to wonder whether to instruct one or not. Anyone facing criminal charges needs a solicitor, all the more so if he has not done whatever he is charged with. Those who cannot afford a solicitor are entitled to have one assigned to them, for which the state will pay.

Legal aid in criminal cases is organised differently than in civil law. Solicitors are selected from a panel of practitioners who have chosen to specialise in this kind of work and are experienced in the procedures. Since such solicitors are not employed by the state, they are free to represent clients who pay them, as well as doing other kinds of legal work. A solicitor owes the same duty to a Legal Aid client as to any other, and a complaint should be made if he does not meet an acceptable standard of service.

It can happen that a solicitor does not come down to the police station because he cannot be contacted. It is not a catastrophe if you have to appear in court the next morning without him. Only minor matters are heard immediately, and in any case, the judge will ask you if you want to apply for legal aid, or if you are instructing your own solicitor. If you are not already on bail, you may need to have someone in court to be your bailsperson. Whoever it is, he or she should know you well, be in a position to ensure, as far as possible, that you will re-appear in court as directed, and be able to prove, there and then, that they can put their hands on whatever sum of money your bail is set at. The usual proof required is a bank or savings book. It is unfair to allow someone to waste a morning in court if he has not been advised of these requirements beforehand. It is a serious matter to be rejected as a bailsperson because it implies that someone is untrustworthy. Another possible source of embarrassment is that he or she is invariably asked if they have ever been convicted of an offence, and their reply is usually checked in garda records.

For most citizens, the only time they will appear in a criminal court is either as witnesses or to go bail for an accused, who is unlikely to warn them of possible difficulties. Many kind-hearted people are upset because they were not told they would be asked questions or required to furnish proof of the accuracy of their replies. Nor were they told they might have to wait around for some time before the case was called. If you put up the bail for a friend or relative who fails to turn up at any stage, the bail is estreated—that is, the sum of money must be paid over to the state, and you will not be given a great deal of time in which to do it. In spite of the fact that they were told this by the court at the time, bailspersons often appear surprised when it happens; they seem to think it was merely a formality. Moreover, it is a matter of record, and they will not be accepted in future as a bailsperson for anyone else. So if you have any doubts about the accused person turning up in court, you should, for your own peace of mind, firmly refuse to enter a bail bond.

The driving of a motor car nearly always entails some encounter with the gardai, however non-contentious, such as getting a licence application form. One is frequently stopped at a check point and asked to produce licence and insurance certificate. If you have to show them at your local station within ten days, you will find it useful to get written confirmation that you have done so. If you have the name and station of the requesting garda, you can telephone or leave a message that you have complied with the law. It may help to avoid a summons being issued for failure to produce the documents, when you have, in fact, done so. Such slip-ups happen too often, to the justifiable annoyance of all concerned. Perhaps, by the next century, all garda stations will have faxes or computer terminals, so that administrative information of this nature is routinely passed on from one station to another. After all, banks have had this kind of facility between their branches for a long time. You know by the look of glazed horror on an official's face that she has looked up your account in some remote seaside branch, which you would have preferred to keep veiled!

Motorists are surprised to receive notices or summonses, frequently relating to parking offences, with the registration number of a car they no longer own, and, therefore, they think they have the perfect defence. It does not follow as day follows night. The obligation to notify the Motor Tax Authority is on the person who is transferring the ownership; there is a specific form to be used for the purpose. It is not right to rely on the buyer to do so, or to accept his statement that he is only buying the vehicle for scrap. Many responsible drivers are horrified to see a car they had long believed reduced to scrap pass them on the road. It is always safer to check with the local authorities about the regulations, rather than take a casual stranger's word.

Some years ago, I read an account in an English newspaper of a cautionary tale which illustrates the wisdom of such advice. A man, spending a quiet evening at home, was visited by the police, who asked him to provide a sample to be tested for alcohol. Since he had not been driving, he refused—reasonably, one might think. A car which he had sold, but had not yet notified the authorities about, had been involved in an accident and failed to stop; his name had emerged as the registered owner. An appeal court subsequently held that the man should have complied with the police request, and it disqualified him from driving. The particular case could not happen here because of the conditions under which a request for such a sample can be made under our law, but no citizen would welcome questions being asked about a vehicle, registered in their name, which was involved in a hit and run, or in an armed robbery, quite apart from the relatively innocent illegal parking. Such a possibility could be avoided by taking steps to get the car out of their name at the time it leaves their possession.

It is a well-established principle that ignorance of the law is no excuse for breaking it. It is not difficult to find out what the law is in relation to the ownership, driving and maintenance of a motor car, nor whose driving is covered under an insurance policy. In the latter instance all you have to do is read the certificate, or check with the insurance company itself, not the broker. However, may you never find out the hard way that it is an offence to be very drunk publicly, to place a bet in a pub, to behave riotously in a theatre or loiter in the streets of Dublin between sunset and eight in the morning, particularly if you are not able to give a good account of yourself! If you are charged with an offence, you must be informed of the nature and category of the offence at the time: you are entitled to know immediately what it is you have been accused of.

The same obligation lies on the police to obey the law as on the public. Where there has been misconduct on the part of a garda officer, a complaint should be made. If it is something you have witnessed, such as undue force being used, or the wrong person arrested, you should not interfere there and then, because you run the risk of being charged with obstructing the police, particularly if there is a row going on at the same time. It is much more effective to call in the next day and report the matter to the local superintendent, or you can make a complaint to the Garda Siochana Complaints Board which is an independent body dealing with complaints from the public against the gardai.

BUYING A HOUSE

5

Of those people lucky enough to be able to buy a house, the majority is even luckier because it will be the only time in their life that they will ever have to talk to a solicitor. Do they absolutely have to? Well, no, they do not; people can do their own conveyancing, as it is called. For most of us, however, the cost is by far the largest sum of (borrowed) money we shall ever get to spend, and we would prefer to place the responsibility of anything going wrong on someone else's shoulders. We feel that it is worth putting together the money to pay a solicitor, on top of all the other money we have had to find.

Conveyancing is primarily concerned with something called 'title'. This means not only a set of documents that will show you are the most recently recorded in a long line of legitimate owners, but that your right to the property is fire-proofed against any attempt by other possible claimants to dislodge you. When you are buying a house, you are buying the title to it, and this can be tricky. It can be threatened by encumbrances, charges, covenants, by-laws, even returning prodigal sons. That is not to say that only a solicitor can master conveyancing. People can learn to do it, like most things, but only a solicitor can be blamed if it all goes wrong. People usually find the house first and then look for a solicitor. It might be better to do it the other way around. The solicitor can tell you about booking deposits, about whether estate agents are bound by what they tell you, and other things to be wary of. He will be delighted to talk to you if you have come about buying a house, and you might as well get all the value you can from him. He is hardly going to charge you for that consultation.

There are all kinds of things the solicitor will be asking you, and you might give the meeting some thought beforehand. You are probably borrowing the money from a building society or a bank. Find out how much you can borrow on foot of the security of the house. It is far less stressful to make a dry run at it, long before you arrive at the stage of spending every Saturday and Sunday afternoon trailing after an estate agent or driving out to the suburbs to be dazzled by the dinky showhouse.

You will find Mr Moneyplus quite relaxed too, when he realises that he does not have to make one of those clear-eyed and immediate decisions for which he is famous in the financial world. In any case, remember that you are only one of a long line of people who have asked him for the loan of money that day, and if nobody had done, he would be out of a job. Besides, he is not going to leave himself short to give it to you. Talk to him about your hopeful plans and the approximate figure you feel the house will cost. He will ask you about your earnings, and what deposit you can afford. Then he will work out a round figure that you will have to repay every month. Enquire about house insurance, too, and what his company's view is on it. Lending institutions usually insist that mortgage protection insurance be taken out so that if the borrower dies, the balance due is covered by the policy.

The fact that you have not found a house yet does not matter, because each loan is in respect of a particular property and will be affected by their surveyor's report on its structural soundness, and its value. The latter is important, because the lender will contribute only a sum based on that value. For instance, even if you think the property is a snip at £40,000, and their man's opinion is that it is not worth more than £36,500, they will offer only the agreed ratio of the latter amount, and you would have to find the extra, provided that they were willing to go ahead on that basis. As the old saying has it: he who pays the piper, calls the tune.

You go back to the dear man, of course, when you come across a house in which you are definitely interested. For some of the meeting you will go over old ground, but the homework will all have been done. You will not be so anxious, particularly if you have your heart set on the house. If it is a second-hand house, this can be a most disappointing time, because of the uncertainty about whether you are going to get it after all. (When you are buying a new house, the usual thing is to sign a building contract with the builder, and at the end of the day you will have a house for an agreed price that looks like the showhouse, on the outside anyway!)

An auction is deadly for the person who aches for a particular house, and for whom the affordable limit has long been set. It is not much fun for the seller, either! Don't be remorseful, thinking that if you had gone the extra £500 it would have been yours. Remember that it is unlikely that the person bidding so relentlessly against you would not also have the same thought. That is why auctioneers like auctions. It will not ease the disappointment at the time, but you will find, as thousands have before you, that when you are eventually settled in a different house entirely, you will feel slightly disloyal that you ever hankered after another.

If you are getting a home loan from a bank, you will have to make arrangements about bridging finance, for instance, with your own bank manager. She will have told you the sum you can write a cheque for, if you are bidding at an auction, because, if your bid is the successful one, you are going to have to pay at least ten per cent of the purchase price there and then. You will have discussed this also if you are going to a building society. It is unchartered territory for most of us, until the day we begin the tentative process of buying a house—which is why, if you are going to employ a solicitor, you should get thinking about him from the start. If he does not know the answers, see that he asks the questions, but stay with him while he does so. He can make a phone call while you are at the other side of the desk, so you can put any other queries that occur as the process is explained. It saves a lot of time, and you get a chance to see exactly how he operates. He may well be moved to go to the auction with you, which should be a great comfort.

If you buy that house, or one further down the road, the solicitor will be dealing with all matters, straight-forward and complex, as the transaction proceeds. This transaction is called conveyancing and it takes experience, patience and—sorry about this—time. There is a process to be gone through and very little of it is visible to the client. That nice serious character, Levin, in *Anna Karenina*, when he was utterly frustrated by legal delays, thought the situation might be bearable if he could understand it all, the way he could understand why people have to approach a booking-office at a railway station in single file. It is a memorable comparison, because if someone is in a queue at any ticket counter, he can see the process before him as people buy tickets or make enquiries and then move away to leave room for the next person. If he cannot see what is happening, he thinks that nothing is.

Some of the law's delays are not unreasonable. Unfortunately, we cannot buy a house like a box of chocolates in a shop. Once you have paid the price, the chocolates are yours—while, in buying a house, you will not be paying the balance of the price until the seller is in a position to hand over the title. However, you have signed a contract and paid a deposit. You have a big stake in seeing that you do not end up with a defective title. Strangely enough, the law puts that duty on you.

The seller does not have to volunteer any information, but he must answer the questions he is asked. These questions are called requisitions on title, and they are compiled only after your solicitor has read the title deeds. His concern is not to see that you get as good a title as the seller has, but to ensure that you get a good title, which may be a different thing. In *Troilus and Cressida*, Shakespeare made fun of those lawyers who prattle on in phrases such as 'fee farm' and 'in witness whereof' but it is not just a smokescreen of self-importance that makes an issue of land being freehold or leasehold. Although the distinction has become blurred, it once made a considerable difference in the manner in which property was transferred. Even if the law has changed, your solicitor has to check what the position was at the particular time any transaction in the chain was completed.

When I was buying a house, it was my lynx-eyed solicitor who spotted that at the time when a previous owner had died, the law that did away with the distinction in the way leasehold and freehold was transferred on death had not been passed and this factor had been overlooked in a vital document. Fortunately, there was someone available to make a new deed. That is just an example of the kind of thing your solicitor will be anxious about. It is not needless mumbo-jumbo; it is important, even if it seems a little ridiculous in a technological age.

Your solicitor will make searches in the Registry of Deeds (as well as other places like the Companies Office or the Law Courts) to see that there are no mortgages or charges, which would mean that someone else would have a better claim on the house than you. It is again because the onus is on the purchaser to satisfy himself that no one other than the seller has a clear title. That is what your solicitor is doing to earn his fee, and following defined procedures so that he is not liable in negligence to you. It usually takes about six weeks. Remember that even if you had the money in your pocket and wanted to be in the house by Sunday, the convenience of the seller must be considered. A closing date is agreed between the parties. Where they agree to an early closing date, the balance of the purchase price is usually put on joint deposit until the legalities are complete, and the seller gets the interest.

It will be nice if you take up residence in a house that the former owners leave with a few light bulbs still in place and the garbage removed. You will think kindly of them all your life if the rose bush is not uprooted in the back garden or if they have not drained the last drop of heating oil from the tank into a jam jar. Gentle reader, there are people who not only remove the light bulbs, but cut the light fitting itself. Avert your mind; do not allow them to spoil your excitement. There is a bright side; those to whom such barbarities have happened are determined if *they* ever sell, which is unlikely, they will leave their much-loved home sparkling and a pot plant on the sill to take away the bare look!

MAKING A WILL

6

Apart from the occasional Agatha Christie story, no one ever died from making a will. Yet many people are very reluctant to do it, even when they have the intention for a long time. It is as if they feared that the very act might draw the attention of the Great Reaper to them. However, if they once sat down, thought about it and did it, they would be pleasantly surprised to find that they never had to think about it again. They would also have the satisfaction that comes from a generous deed, but in this case, they will continue to own and enjoy whatever they have given away.

Solicitors do not make the connection of wills with death, but then lawyers are persons, according to an American jurist, who can hold an idea in their minds that is intimately connected with something else, yet give no thought to that other something. So, in the same breath, a solicitor may tell a client that he has never seen her look so well and ask her if she has made her will yet! If you tell a solicitor you want to make a will, he will make no connection with that wish and the current state of your health. In fact, he will be delighted, having seen the unnecessary chaos that has resulted in many instances where people have not made a will.

We all know of such cases and the confusion and difficulties, not to speak of expense, to those left behind. We have tut-tutted at the lack of foresight—and never apply it to ourselves. One time, my uncle was ill, and a concerned friend worried about whether he had made a will: 'I wouldn't like to see Tom going without having his affairs settled.' Both men lived on for several years, but it was the fussy friend who died intestate.

There is no point in thinking that it is pretentious to make a will unless you are well off. There are probably things we would like certain friends to enjoy after we are no longer able to enjoy them ourselves. If you own a house, furniture, a bicycle, a bank account, a dog, you have something to leave. And next week, you may win the Lotto.

Everyone is pleased to be remembered in a will. It has little to do with value but a lot to do with gratitude. Sometimes, the impulse is to wrap up the particular object and present it there and then, just for the pleasure of giving it in person, so to speak.

There are wills that are made without legal help. There are forms available, and the instructions are not hard to understand. But wills, or rather the interpretation of them, can be tricky, especially when the particular individual is not around to explain what he meant exactly. Remember poor Captain Boyle in *Juno and the Paycock* and all the new prosperity that came crashing down, because the word 'cousins' in the will did not mean what it was intended to? A will is a legal document—heaven knows nothing is more so—and if you have doubts, then you probably would prefer to talk to a solicitor.

If you want to make a number of bequests—which is what a gift is called in a will—then you should be getting out pencil and paper and assembling your thoughts.

There is some property that cannot be bequeathed by will. Anything owned jointly by two or more persons passes automatically to the survivor. Life interests, such as a house that was given to someone for their lifetime, cannot be given away. Nor can you bequeath an object, which you have already given to someone else, or which you have only the loan of. In other words, if there is a legal prior claim by another person, then it is not yours to give in the first place.

A house is different, because, if mortgaged, the beneficiary i.e. the person who inherits, will take it subject to the terms of the agreement with the building society or bank. Most people, however, will have a mortgage protection policy, which has already been mentioned.

When we finally get down to making our will with a solicitor, most of us have no difficulty with the big things, like the house, the car, the gifts of money. We feel self-conscious when it comes to the chat about our small treasures. We blushingly explain that the teapot we are leaving to a favourite sister is not part of the Derrynaflan Hoard, but a battered, brown earthenware job that she has always wanted for her own. And then, somehow, it becomes impossible to explain about Dad's old walking stick, and we abandon the whole exercise.

I have been trying to think of a way we could keep control of this process, and yet make it effective. Why not ask the solicitor if you could leave a direction to your executors (about whom I shall explain shortly) that they are to distribute certain items according to your wishes, which are written out in a list? It means you could write it out in your own time, and you would have the pleasure of adding to it from time to time—and perhaps the occasional satisfaction of subtraction! There may be a way in which small articles could be accounted for, that would be flexible, but since you also need to make sure that your wishes are effective, you would certainly require proper legal advice.

Executors have been mentioned; it would cause difficulty if you made a will without appointing at least one. This is the person who will carry out the terms of your will. It is not a bad idea to consider two executors, one of them a solicitor, the other a relative. It makes for convenience, since the solicitor will be dealing with the legal requirements and the relative can speak for the family interest, especially if there are young children to be taken care of. In fairness to everyone, it is a matter that should be given a great deal of thought. Above all, you must ask the person you choose for her prior consent. It is appalling not to do so, and even though, in such a case, she can refuse to act when the time comes, many people feel obliged to take it on from a sense of responsibility, but they also feel considerable resentment. All of this is avoidable by simply first asking them for their permission.

Their responsibilities are laid down by law; in effect, they act as your trusted agent in carrying out your instructions. Apart from that, they can be given specific powers under any particular will, some of which may be confidential. It is useful to bear in mind, if it is desired to benefit someone, without necessarily telling the whole world.

A will can be changed at any time, and this is sometimes done by means of a codicil, which is an alteration or addition and must be witnessed in the same way as a will—as this nation knows, at the cost of the Hugh Lane pictures! One beneficiary who can only be written out of a will in very exceptional circumstances is a spouse. A husband or a wife has a legal right to one-third of the other's estate, if there are children, and a half, if there are none. Children do not have automatic rights of inheritance; that would be a matter for a court to decide in relation to any child's age and circumstances. Most married people make simple wills leaving everything to their spouse, but anyone thinking of something a bit more complicated should certainly consult a solicitor. In any event, it is one relatively small outlay during the course of our life to ensure we do not leave chaos and confusion after us; or worse still, that our small store is not wasted away on lawyers' fees, instead of being of benefit to those we intended to help.

BEREAVEMENT

7

When someone close to us dies, our mind will certainly not leap to questions about the legal aspects or obligations. However, they will have to be considered in the days that follow, so it is perhaps better to acquaint ourselves with a few general principles when all around us are in the whole of their health.

The family solicitor, where there is one, should be contacted, since the deceased may have left instructions about a preferred place of burial, or organ donation, in his or her will, which would need to be ascertained as soon as possible, although most people let their family know any wishes of that nature well in advance. Of course, you may not know if there is a will. The original is often left with a solicitor or a bank, and a plain copy kept with other papers, but one does see frequent advertisements asking for information about lost wills.

One of the most painful situations is where someone is dying who has not made a will, and the family knows that this was not his intention, but feel it is impossible to talk about it. It is not that they are afraid to be thought grasping, but that the link between serious illness and a will would now be too obvious. It is hardly fair to ask the doctor or the solicitor to discuss the matter, since it is truly the individual's own business, and there is, after all, no obligation to make a will. Naturally, the only acceptable approach is one which has to do with the peace of mind of the person himself, who may be worried about his affairs and wanting to talk to someone. Perhaps a family member or a very close friend might reassure him that there is no difficulty if he wants to talk to a solicitor—or if he does not want to—and the matter be left there. It is a dilemma that frequently occurs, and there is no ready answer to it. Relatives can only take whatever steps they think possible in the circumstances; more often than not they reluctantly conclude there is nothing they can do.

An intestacy is what occurs when a person dies leaving no will, and the estate will be divided among the next-of-kin according to the degree of kindred. Where there is a spouse and children, the former gets two-thirds and the remainder is divided among the children. If there are no children, the widow or widower is entitled to all the estate. Similarly, the parents are the inheritors, if the deceased left no spouse or children; brothers and sisters inherit if the parents are dead and so on. More remote relatives are only entitled to a distribution of the property when there is no immediate family.

Whether or not someone dies leaving a will, their estate passes to a legal personal representative in the first instance. This is the executor under the will, who takes out a grant of probate. If the person died intestate—that is, not having made a will—then letters of administration are granted to the nearest relative. There is no difference in the degree of duty for the personal representatives, no matter how appointed. They hold the property on trust for those entitled to it, either under the terms of the will, or under the law of intestate succession. They gather together the assets of the deceased, pay the funeral costs and any other lawful debts and distribute the remainder. Where property has not been transferred a year after the death, application can be made to court to require the representative to produce an inventory and account of the deceased's estate, or to make an order ensuring that the land is transferred to the person entitled.

When beneficiaries are being told that they have been left a legacy, they will be given a copy of the will or, at least, of that portion which relates to them. In any case, once the will has been proved—that is, admitted to probate, it becomes a public document and can be inspected by anyone in the probate registry on payment of a small fee. Apart from the principal Probate Office at the Four Courts, there are district probate registries around the country and information on their location can be got at the nearest court office. You can also take out a grant of probate or administration as a personal applicant. Any executor or administrator can do this: it is not means tested, the fees are very reasonable, and a leaflet giving all the necessary information is available at all probate registries, or you could write to the Probate Office at the Four Courts.

On the other hand, people who are used to dealing with solicitors usually leave the administration of a relative's estate in their hands. If the matter is contentious, such as a disputed will or a complicated claim against the estate, it is difficult to see how one could proceed without legal advice. A notice of *caveat* is often entered to prevent a will being admitted until litigation is disposed of, or a quarrel resolved.

A person's estate remains liable for debts incurred when he was alive, and may also be liable for damages, perhaps from a motor accident in which he was at fault, provided the proceedings were issued within certain time limits. Property acquired after he made his last will is included as part of his residuary estate, and would pass under a gift expressed on the lines of 'all the rest, residue and remainder to so-and-so'. If there was no such phrase to catch it, then property, not specifically mentioned, is distributed as in an intestate succession. There are many instances where a poor relative has worked for years without pay, on the promise of being 'remembered in the will' and, in fact, is left nothing. There may very well be a claim in debt against the estate, and it would be well worth talking to a solicitor in such a case.

A spouse is the person most often appointed as executor or will be the personal representative where there is an intestacy. She or he will therefore be dealing with the solicitor as both client and main beneficiary. The administration of estates gives rise to much irritation between solicitor and client because of delay, lack of information and the general lassitude into which it frequently seems to sink. For a trenchant description of the effect of the latter, we need look no further than Dickens's *Bleak House* which should be required reading for all lawyers every three years. While we are waiting for that to come about, what can you do, as personal representative? It will save time if you undertake to get as much information together, yourself, as you can. Get all the bills, payslips, or dividend vouchers, photo-copy them and bring the copies to the solicitor. You can find out when the papers will be ready for your signature, and what arrangements will be made with the bank regarding the executor's account. Give instructions to be told when the grant is issued by the Probate Office and what banks or other institutions it must be first sent to for noting.

If any difficulties arise in the administration, you must be told without delay, because you are the one responsible, in law, for the estate, and for any taxes that have to be paid. You should be told the estimated time of each stage and make regular enquiries about progress. That way, the affairs of the dead do not get buried under those of the living, and therefore more insistent, clients.

Solicitors should themselves realise that they are more frequently judged in this situation by the public, for good or ill, than they think. How often one hears as a recommendation of one of them, 'I was very impressed with the efficient and sensitive way she dealt with my father's estate when he died: the family had no complaints whatsoever.'

MARRIAGE

8

Marriage has to do with legal status. Many of us fail to grasp that simple reality. We confuse it with love, fantasy, regret, fidelity, religion and wedding cake. It may involve one or more of those ingredients, and many others, but none of them is necessary to the state of being married. To enter into a contract of marriage, which is recognised by the law of the land, is to change one's status, in the same way as we do when we reach eighteen or are imprisoned or lose our sanity. We engage the mechanism of the law in a different gear than we have done previously.

One of the main reasons for the confusion is religion. Because many people get married in a religious ceremony, they have difficulty distinguishing between the elements in the contract that are spiritual and those that are strictly legal. The fact that they seem to merge in the one action adds to the misunderstanding. Moreover, the requirements that are necessary in any particular religion to make a valid marriage may not be the same under the law.

A couple who are legally entitled to marry make promises of exclusive commitment to each other and mutual support; that exchange and acceptance of promises is recorded in writing. A copy of the record is registered in an official book, and this registration of marriage is what makes it recognised by the state. It will be necessary to produce a certificate of that record whenever proof of a marriage is needed. Of course, I can whisper whatever secret vows I wish, but if I want my marriage to be recognised by the state, I must enter into the contract openly, before a third party, who is authorised to witness it taking place and to record it for registration. Furthermore, the marriage must be held at a place licensed for that purpose.

Most religions take a strong interest in the marriage of the members of their faith. They have individual procedures and rules. They also have their own ritual. So, for the sake of convenience, ministers of religion are recognised as persons entrusted with the duty of carrying out the state's rules regarding registration. If they are going to do this, they must ensure that the couple are entitled to marry under the law of the state. So they are performing a dual function: as a minister of religion, and as the servant of the state, for the purposes of registration.

It is easier to understand the legal element when the event takes place in a registry office. The promises made are just as solemn and as binding as in a church, but the registrar, who witnesses the contract and registers the marriage, does so solely on behalf of the civil authority. Many people seem to have a notion that a civil ceremony makes for a second-class kind of marriage, yet within the society regulated by laws that regard married people as distinct from single persons, it is the *civil* content that determines their status. The same confusions do not occur in France, where you must have a separate civil marriage, regardless of whatever other wedding ceremony takes place.

You may marry if both parties are over eighteen, are not already married to an existing spouse, and have given the required notice either to the local Registrar of Marriages or to their minister of religion. If you are under eighteen but over sixteen, you will require the consent of your parents to marry. A divorced person may marry in Ireland, provided the divorce is recognised by the law here. You should certainly get a solicitor's advice in such an event.

Bigamy is a very serious crime, and it is a matter of amazement to many lawyers how lightly some people embark upon it. It is unusual, in that you can be prosecuted in a country other than the one in which you went through the bigamous marriage. You can also be prosecuted long afterwards, and it does not matter that the original spouse has died in the meantime. Its discovery not only leads to endless legal repercussions in loss of property and status but, worse still, it causes unbearable pain in families. Anyone who takes part as a witness to a bigamous marriage, in the full knowledge that one of the parties was already married, might have trouble explaining their own position in any subsequent proceedings. It is far better to get proper advice on the possibility of exploring other alternatives, but it is useless consulting a solicitor unless he is to be given truthful information. Even if he is not able to help, you will not have peace of mind if you close your eyes and hope for the best. It is too much to risk for the sake of a sham legal ceremony and a party: why not just have the party?

While a divorced person may marry in Ireland provided that the particular divorce is recognised by our law, it would be a matter of confirmation, in the first place, by the local Registrar of Marriages (see page 89). If you are not satisfied with the Registrar's decision, you will probably consider taking legal advice, possibly with a view to making an application to the court. If so, the solicitor will require a great deal of information as well as an official copy of the decree of divorce. The information would include the relevant law of the country, the domicile of the parties to the original marriage, and precise dates. The law of domicile, a different concept from residence, is very complicated, has varying interpretations in every jurisdiction, and is impossible to explain. This is said by way of warning before the invitations go out. If it was not accepted by the Registrar, it is probable that there was something unusual about the particular decree, so that it is bound to take a considerable time before the matter is ready to be presented in court.

We could take a brief look at some of the legal consequences that follow from the marriage day, and whether any of them are matters that the couple might wish to examine more closely with a solicitor. You may be the kind of person who is convinced that this is one union that will last, but who might also think that those who take sensible precautions against catastrophe thus ensure that it will never happen. After all, nobody marries with divorce in mind, yet divorce exists. You could reasonably think that in this mood of love and trust, it would be better to provide for the extremely faint possibility of things not turning out well, rather than do it when the mood would be one of remorse and revenge.

Women's Aid launched a prototype of a pre-marriage contract some years ago which was very well thought-out. It was concerned with the development of the person within a marriage, and respect for the essential individuality of the parties. It was a counsel of perfection, naturally. Were it to be followed exactly, there would be no need for pre-nuptial agreements in the legal sense, which are primarily concerned with property. Such agreements are frowned upon as being contrary to the public good in that they anticipate the possibility of the marriage not lasting a lifetime. It is unlikely that any court here would enforce their terms. Of course if it were to come to a court case, it would be obvious that the agreement, like the marriage, had not worked out! In any case under the new judicial separation legislation, the court, in the cases which come before it, oversees the arrangements concerning children and the disposition of property, in the absence of agreement.

One legal document that is rendered useless by marriage is a will. The only will that survives marriage is one that is made in anticipation of it. If you say that you are making your will with your forthcoming marriage in mind, you do not have to make another one when married. It is a practical matter which is worth some thought, at a stage when a couple are acquiring bits and pieces in anticipation of setting up a home together. If you decide you want to put your wishes down in black and white, you could have a solicitor draw up simple wills—and never have to give it another thought.

Another factor that comes into play in marriage is the legal concept of presumption. There are several presumptions which reflected the status of married women in the past. A legal presumption is the acceptance that a state of affairs exists unless there is evidence to the contrary; in other words, a working hypothesis. It was presumed that a husband was responsible for his wife's debts. That could be rebutted by showing that such debts were incurred in the course of her business, which she operated independently of him. If he were to put property in her name, it is presumed that he intended her to have the benefit of it. He could not get it back against her wishes, unless he were able to prove that he had positively not so intended. There was a presumption that if a couple committed a crime together, the wife had acted under the coercion of the husband: there was not any presumption in his favour. When the hen-pecked Mr Bumble in *Oliver Twist* was told that the law assumed his wife had acted under his direction, he blurted out, '. . . the law is a ass'.

As women emerge from their husbands' shadows, the core idea of a married woman's total dependency has been considerably weakened. She can be sued separately for debt; she can enter into hire-purchase agreements, and a husband no longer has to sign his wife's income tax return. There is one sensible idea remaining: a husband can take out a life insurance policy, which is payable to his wife on production of his death certificate. In many households where the man is the sole wage-earner, this means that the widow does not have to wait until the legal niceties are completed before she gets any money to support herself and her family.

Most couples now buy their houses jointly. It is by far the most sensible way to do it. If one partner dies, the property passes immediately to the other, again without a grant of administration having to be taken out first. If there was any question of death duties, they will be halved on the value of the house. If the property is not already in joint names, and you wish it were, ask your solicitor to do it; it is a simple deed and the stamp duty will only be one per cent of half the value.

In recent years there has been much better protection for the spouse who has no legal ownership. Where the house is, or has been, the family home, then the one who owns it cannot sell or mortgage it without the consent of the other. This also applies where the deeds are lodged as security for a loan. It applies even if the house was owned by one of the partners long before a marriage that was short-lived. It can result in unexpected difficulties where a spouse has decamped several years before and the other wants to sell the house.

What else does marriage change? Not your name, anyway, unless this is what you want. On that subject, we are all entitled to call ourselves anything we please, as long as we do not intend to deceive others. We may be socially embarrassed by the antics of our spouse, but we are not legally responsible for the consequences of his or her behaviour unless our conduct would reasonably lead a third party to that conclusion. If this sounds vague, then it is necessarily so, since all the circumstances would have to be examined in each case.

If your partner is planning some project which involves money, and yourself in a peripheral way, then you should talk to a solicitor if one is already engaged. If not, get some proper advice. To do this is not asking for trouble. If the undertaking is not able to withstand a cool examination, it might be time to reconsider it. It may very well be that both parties are prepared to risk everything in this exciting new venture, but each should be given the same amount of information about his or her liabilities.

UNHAPPY DIFFERENCES

9

We have seen that the status of being married is a legal one, so the law is necessarily invoked in any alteration of that status. It is the ideal of every man and woman, that, in the event of things going wrong, they walk away in peace, with their self-respect intact. Sadly, it remains an ideal. Perhaps it is possible for the saints among us, but a saint might endure the unhappiness with never a cross word exchanged with the life partner. Even without sainthood, but merely with goodwill, it should not be too difficult to make amicable arrangements about the children, houses, school holidays, and to say—'You take this, I'll take that and we will draw lots for the things we can't agree about.' But goodwill in these circumstances is as unlikely as sainthood. People part in anger, not in cool calculation. All that we can hope is that the immediate anger will pass swiftly enough to allow for some level-headed planning. When it is clear to you that a situation exists which you are not prepared to tolerate, the next step is to consider your options.

If there is a threat to your family's welfare, the most direct and quickest option is a barring order. The procedure is put in motion by making an application in the local office of the District Court. A summons is issued to the other spouse to attend court on a certain date, when the application will be heard by a judge. It is usually preceded by a protection order, in which the court directs one spouse not to threaten, molest or frighten the other, or any member of the family. The gardai have power to arrest without a warrant, if such an order is broken. The arrested person is brought before an ordinary public court to be tried, although matters relating to the issue of barring or maintenance orders are heard in private.

The barring procedure is a drastic measure, because it means putting somebody out of their own home, and there is no question of it being granted automatically. It is a step that is only taken in very grave circumstances and where there appears to be no other alternative. A court does not take kindly to any attempted abuse of the process, such as to vent a momentary spleen, or to get rid of someone who has simply become a nuisance. Remember too that, except in rare cases, a barring order is of its nature temporary. It exists to provide relief in an oppressive situation, and should never be considered as a makeshift divorce.

If there are deep divisions between husband and wife—what lawyers call 'unhappy differences'—they should consider a separation agreement. This is a contract in which all the issues are agreed between them and set down in writing; they are bound by its terms, as in any other contract. It is very unlikely that such a document could be drawn up without legal advice, and each spouse should be separately represented. It is extremely painful to have to talk to a third party about one's marriage. It goes against every instinct to discuss adverse feelings about a person to whom loyal support was the strict convention for years, no matter what the private doubts. Many people put up with nearly intolerable situations rather than face such an ordeal, and only do so when they feel driven to it. It would be useful, also, to write down why you think your marriage has come to an end. It would help to clear your mind and calm some of your worst fears. When you do talk to a solicitor, it will be easier to remember what you want to tell him, and prevent you becoming too upset and even incoherent.

However, you must first find the right solicitor. There was a time when few lawyers in Ireland dealt with matrimonial disputes, but the obvious increase in demand has led many more to specialise in family law. The Incorporated Law Society of Ireland will suggest some names if you enquire. It is essential for your peace of mind that you have one you like and trust, who will be reliable and give you all the information you need. He will also have the common sense to realise that the person you married was the one you chose from all the others, and, no matter how badly things have turned out, to demean your husband or wife is to demean you. Things are difficult enough for you without having to endure denigrating or smart-alecky remarks.

If it looks as if you are going to be caught up in heart-wrenching and protracted wrangling, which will wear you down, then your solicitor is going to become your lifeline to sanity and the promise of a brighter future. He has got to be very good. If you have negative feelings after the first consultation, then there is no reason on earth to stay with him. On the other hand, baring your soul to a succession of unsympathetic persons would be a fearful prospect. So begin by deciding that you are in the driving seat and he is obliged to take his instruction from *you*. You are in a better position to do this if you have first thought everything through.

Tell him about the matters that you consider relevant and those you do not wish to pursue. He should not ask you questions that you are obviously reluctant to answer, without convincing you of their necessity. This may sound aggressive, but it does not have to be. Unfortunately, today, when ordinary good manners are no longer ordinary, it is often our own behaviour which indicates to others how we wish to be treated by them. As regards most solicitors, such dire warnings are superfluous, but it is something to keep in mind, in case we reject a solicitor out of hand, and yet hear his praises sung for years afterwards.

Many people hope that when a solicitor's letter is received, the seriousness of the situation will dawn on the other partner, who will mend his or her ways, or move out. Mostly, it does not work that way. Instead, there may be hoots of derision or a baffling silence; it may be weeks before there is any reaction. It can indeed be disappointing, but it is better to be prepared for the fact that no progress may be discernible until proceedings are issued. Once a case is set down with a date for hearing, even the ostrich with the longest neck knows that it is time to get the sand out of its eyes, and its feathers in some kind of order. Judges have a lot of cases to get through in any term, and will certainly not allow endless adjournments so that one of the parties can drag things out.

This is one of the most trying times to live through and it is important that clients are given the fullest information by their solicitors. There are tactics that can seem like psychological warfare to individuals who already had to brace themselves to bring the proceedings in the first place. Once that course is decided upon, the time scale should be discussed in detail with the solicitor. It is up to you to consent to any extension of time in which documents from the other side are to be filed. If parties have been given a reasonable time in which to respond, they cannot feel unfairly flustered by an insistence that they comply with a time limit. It is, of course, a matter for the court to grant adjournments and extensions of time, but that does not mean that what either party has to say on the issue is not first heard before the decision is made.

In the recent past, the grounds of application for a judicial separation have become more practical; for example, that the behaviour of one spouse is such that the other could not be expected to live with him or her. There are also grounds based on various intervals of time in which the couple has lived apart, or where the court is satisfied that a normal marital relationship no longer exists. These grounds are very wide, and it will be of considerable interest to see how the courts interpret them, as time goes by. One thing we do know now, however, and that is that the parties to any such court application will not be free to re-marry as a result. It is a judicial separation, not a divorce.

Proceedings may be taken in either the Circuit Court or the High Court. Before the action is heard, your solicitor will talk to you about the possibility of reconciliation, and will tell you about the agencies who could help if you were willing to try. He will discuss a mediated separation on an agreed basis, or whether a separation agreement can be negotiated. No matter how angry you are, please listen to him carefully, and cooperate with him in the discussion. He is required to do this by law, and in due course, he will have to certify to the court that he has done so. The court, itself, will also consider these possibilities before embarking on a hearing of the matter. Any communication between the parties and a counsellor or mediator is private, and nothing arising from it can be given as evidence in a court. Arrangements concerning children, the family home and finance, are also considered by the court before a decree of judicial separation is granted. Matrimonial and family cases are heard in private; only the parties and their lawyers are present with the judge and registrar. Efforts are made to create an informal atmosphere by discarding the usual wigs and gowns.

The Family Mediation Service, whose address is given on page 90, although based in Dublin is available, free of charge, to any couple who want to use it. It offers the opportunity for those who have agreed to separate, to enter into negotiations, assisted by a trained mediator, with a view to coming to agreement on a wide spectrum of issues which have to be decided, when a marriage breaks up. The object is not to reconcile them nor does it necessarily operate to exclude solicitors. In fact, proceedings may be adjourned while the mediation process is continuing. The terms that are agreed upon may, in fact, result in a legal separation agreement. It is not necessary that the parties are amicably disposed to each other; probably a lot of hurt, anger and disillusion has to be expressed before the couple can begin to make decisions about the future.

Mediation gives one a chance to do this; legal proceedings certainly will not. They each, of course, carry the hope that there will be some resolution of the difficulties in the end. Perhaps, also, there will be an extension of the free mediation service to centres outside Dublin in the near future, which would save the public a considerable amount of travelling.

There are other agencies that you can approach for advice before coming to any decision to take action. All are staffed by qualified persons, well experienced in listening to the difficulties that are encountered in a marriage.

There is a list of addresses that might be helpful on page 90. Do not be put off going because of the cost; free counselling is available for those who cannot afford to pay. Individuals, as well as couples, have derived enormous strength and comfort from the chance to talk to someone sympathetic, whose only purpose is to listen and to counsel.

LIVING TOGETHER

10

While many couples live together because, for some reason, they cannot marry, others choose to do so because it does not seem to them that entering a formal marriage will add anything to their relationship, other than form. And, as elsewhere in life, it is fine until something goes wrong. Then people ask: 'What does the law say about it?' In this case, very little.

If the term common law wife/husband ever meant anything more concrete than a simple description at common law, it has been eroded long ago. Marriage is a legal institution from which certain duties flow, and so do rights, which historically operated to protect married women. The quaintly named widow's paraphernalia, which included her bed, cooking utensils and some clothes, could not be claimed by her husband's creditors, if he died in debt. The cost of her mourning weeds was one of the first charges on his estate, after the funeral expenses. Modern laws no longer distinguish between husband and wife in respect of the family home or the duties owed to each other, because these would offend against the concept of equal rights between the sexes, but in any case, none of these laws applies to a couple who are not married to each other.

It is not that they do not have any rights, one against the other, but they are personal rights, which do not spring from any bond between them that is recognised in law—apart from matters to do with their children, if they have any. They have one advantage—they are free to enter into an agreement on what is to happen should they split up, something a married couple cannot do, as we have seen, since it is regarded as counter-productive to the ideal of marriage. It is a pity that so few avail of the opportunity to make a simple agreement, perhaps believing that it is more legal clap-trap, which they do not need any more than they need the formality of a marriage certificate. Surely it is not impossible to be wise before the event, for a change. An hour or so of calm discussion is preferable to a bitter row about possessions later, leading sometimes to accusations of larceny being made in a criminal court. The couple, whose love was forever, are now arguing about who owns the U2 album, not because they are silly people, but because they are hurt. There was a great song from some years ago called 'You're moving out today' which gives a vivid idea of the kind of items that have to be parcelled out, when what used to be called 'a love nest' is being taken apart, twig by painful twig.

When friends or acquaintances who are not romantically involved share a house or a flat, a row about possessions rarely happens, because what belongs to each person is clear. Even if they buy a television together, they are free to say something like, 'If we split up later, one of us can buy out the other's share', without anyone getting upset. No one would dream of saying it to someone they are in love with. More's the pity, though; it might save lawyers' fees later on.

Engaged couples who buy a house together will discover from their solicitor that the law regulates, to some extent, how their individual contributions to the purchase price are to be assessed, if the house is sold. When they are getting a loan, they will have to make declarations that they are single, and moreover, that they were not engaged to marry someone else during the three preceding years. An engagement means that an offer of marriage was accepted; it does not necessarily include a ring and an announcement in the newspaper. If you have had another fiancé within that time, it will not prevent you buying a house with your present intended. All that is entailed is a further declaration about any possible contributions to the purchase.

Joint owners who are married to other people may encounter initial difficulties in getting a loan, simply because a spouse has certain rights in the family home, and lending agencies are understandably anxious to protect their security, which is your house. It is a complicated matter and you should get legal advice before you agree to buy a house with another person.

There is great bewilderment and sadness experienced often in partnerships where no will has been made. Even if a couple has lived together for more than thirty years, the survivor will not be entitled to any part of the estate, as of right. The family, immediate or distant, will inherit. If the deceased has no kin, the state will take it all. If you think it unfair, remember that it was totally within the power of the departed, at any time during those long, happy years, to make a simple will, which might have, at least, preserved a home for the partner left behind. Sadly the reverse happens far too often. A will cannot be made for someone after he is dead. If he did not make one while he was alive, it must be assumed that he did not want to, which is the hardest of all to accept. I do not apologise for repeating what I said in Chapter 6: make a will—it is not at all difficult.

You would certainly need to talk to a solicitor to get precise advice about what is called 'testamentary freedom', that is to the extent to which you are entitled to dispose of your property as you please. It is obvious that this depends on each person's marital and parental status and what kind of property they own. There is no reason to feel embarrassed in referring to your concern to see that someone, to whom you do not have a legal obligation, is provided for. Solicitors are there to advise clients, in the law as well as what is in their best interests: they are not there to be shocked or titillated by anything they are told during a consultation. They are, moreover, accustomed to hearing all kinds of things in the course of a day. So if you are in such a situation, and have it on your mind to do something, but you do not know what, then go and talk to a solicitor and get proper advice, without further delay. Remember, also, that you can go to a solicitor anywhere in Ireland; it does not have to be the one who lives next door.

Children of unmarried parents are in a far better position now than they were in the past. They have the same rights of inheritance as other children. Their father can apply to be appointed joint guardian with their mother. This goes a great way to providing reassurance to the parents, if they are not free to marry each other, and to the child concerned, particularly in later years. It is a procedure that helps to fill a gap in our law, where there is no formal method by which an acknowledgment of fatherhood is made, and which in other jurisdictions has considerably softened the trauma that a child might have suffered from 'illegitimacy'. It must be borne in mind that it is a matter for a court to decide. A single mother is the sole guardian of her child and married parents are joint guardians. That position can only be changed by will or the order of a court. In any decision concerning guardianship, a judge will be guided by the perception of the child's best interest. That is not merely an admirable principle; it is the law. Much needless anxiety would be spared if it were realised that the rights of the parents are not the primary consideration. So that while in recent years unmarried fathers have been given a right to apply to the court for access, custody or joint guardianship, these are not rights to be set against the mother's. Whether he is to be allowed any of these facilities will be decided in the light of what is best for the child.

Legal aid—the services of a solicitor—is provided free by the Civil Legal Aid Board. The solicitors there are very hardworking and competent, but they have not the resources to cope with all the calls on them. Family law cases form the bulk of their work, but they can only represent married persons, since the law applies only to families based on marriage. If a potentially violent situation happens in a non-marital home, the party who is at risk has the same right to the protection of the law as any other citizen. She can make a complaint to the gardai, or take out a summons for breach of the peace. While the District Court can bind over the offender and make the order subject to certain conditions, it is not possible to order someone to vacate his own house; that can only be done in the context of a barring order, which applies only to married people, as we have seen. However, experience has shown that when these matters surface in court, quite often solutions are worked out with the help of the probation or social service. The local housing officer might also be of help, especially if there are children involved. If the matter was very serious or there was an element of urgency, you could apply to the Circuit Court for an injunction restraining the other party. This is a serious and complicated process, for which you would certainly require the services of a solicitor. You would need to give him very full instructions, so that he can draw up the affidavits and get the matter into court as quickly as possible. It is not a matter of having to lie on the difficult bed you have made for yourself, even if society is more protective of marriage than of looser arrangements.

The Federation of Services for Unmarried Parents and their Children is a national body which provides extensive information on all these aspects and many others in a series of very helpful leaflets, and also maintains a country-wide referral service. The address is given on page 91. An unmarried parent or an interested relative, who was about to take legal advice, would still find the Information Pack supplied by the Federation to be of great assistance in understanding the changes that have been recently made in the law.

CHILDREN

11

Perhaps the idea of a child having personal legal rights is strange to a parent, and also that he or she may have a duty to pursue them on behalf of the child, regardless of personal inclination—for example, where a child has suffered some injury that may or may not have a long-term effect. Should an award be made as a result of a legal action, it will be invested under court supervision, and any payments out will be solely for the child's benefit during infancy. Equally, any offer of settlement must be approved by the court. In the days of the Irish Hospital Sweepstakes, a father or mother who bought a ticket in the baby's name to bring good luck, would sometimes be astounded to find that it was their child who was the millionaire! The law presumed that they wanted to benefit their offspring, not themselves. It is only in recent years that it has become legal to buy a Prize Bond for the child, and in the happy event of a win, there are regulations governing the application for payment, which would be a matter for the administration.

Infancy used to mean the years before twenty-one—'the coming of age'. This particular milestone was changed in 1985, but not in every respect. Young people of eighteen can vote, enter contracts or receive money that was invested for their benefit, but it is not a substitution of the age of eighteen for that of twenty-one generally. It is always safer to make enquiries about any specific case, rather than make a rash assumption.

Every child has a constitutional right to primary education, and a parent can be prosecuted under the School Attendance Acts for not sending him to school, and fined; a child may be educated at home if he is getting a certain minimum education. This right does not mean that the state has a duty to provide primary education at a school of the parent's choice, as is sometimes believed. Another right a child has is to be maintained by its parents, but they are rarely prosecuted for failure to do so. What usually happens is that the child is taken into care by the local authority, or it may be left to the mother to pursue the father and breadwinner on the child's behalf.

Are parents liable for the wrongful acts of their children? Once a child reaches the age of seven, he is regarded as being responsible for his actions, both civil and criminal. In regard to the latter, this means he is considered to be old enough to be tried for an offence. Children under fifteen may be questioned only in the presence of a parent or guardian, unless one cannot be found, and it is also preferred that parents be in court for the hearing.

Whether a person could be made responsible in damages for the civil wrongdoing of his child—for example, causing an accident through negligence—would be a matter of proving that he had effective control over his son's or daughter's actions at the time, or should have had. However, what might determine the likelihood of such an action being attempted would be the financial standing of the parent, whether he is what lawyers call 'a good mark for damages', so that we can take it that a prospective litigant will look more closely at the incident if the child's parent is a banker, rather than a school teacher.

When one is sued as the parent of the child, there is little choice except to take the matter to a solicitor and discuss the question of liability. If, on the other hand, you are the one to have been injured in your person or property through a child's act, and you seek legal advice, you may find that caution is recommended because of the difficulty of obtaining sufficient proof. When any court proceedings are initiated they cost money, which may never be recovered, regardless of the loss or injury suffered. It is a very strong reason for listening closely to a solicitor when he is outlining not only the burden of proof you have to discharge in making your claim, but the amount of money that you stand to lose if you are unsuccessful at the end of the day. This applies where any court action is contemplated, no matter how much right there is in your cause.

Custody and guardianship are aspects of adult-child relationships which have precise legal connotations and it is important to distinguish between them. A guardian represents a child in legal proceedings, and also makes the decisions on its welfare, upbringing and education. It does not necessarily mean that they live in the same house. In the overwhelming majority of cases, the parents are the joint guardians of their children. However, another person may be appointed by the court or by the will of a deceased parent, in which latter case, he or she is called a 'testamentary guardian' and represents the child in respect of whatever benefit is acquired under the will. Similarly, the court will define the duties of any guardian that it appoints.

Where parents are living apart, and the court, on application, awards custody of children to one parent, it will usually allow the other parent to spend time with the children; this is called access and the conditions are set

out by the judge. Ideally these matters are arranged amicably between the parties, but where that cannot be done,
the court will do so, on terms it considers to serve the
best interests of the child. Where the mother has custody—
which is customary if the children are very young—
arrangements must be made for the children to visit
their father, or he them, at certain times. It has at least
as much to do with the children's rights as the parents'.
If you are in this kind of situation, it may save painful
arguments with your solicitor to accept, when he points
these strictures out, that he is reflecting the decisions
that judges are making every day in attempting to ensure
that the welfare of the child is of paramount importance.
Parents, who are accustomed to making decisions on
behalf of their children, naturally find it difficult to allow
someone else take over that role. It must be underlined
that parents, under the law, are the primary guardians of
their children, and normally, a court will only intervene
if there is disagreement or incompetence.

The concept of adoption is different from that of
guardianship, because an adopted child acquires new
parents, as if it had been born to them, and becomes
part of another family. While some adoptive parents may
very well talk to a solicitor beforehand, there is no call to
be legally represented in most adoptions. Besides, many
adoptions are by a married couple for adoption of the
woman's child and this procedure is quite straightforward.
A great deal of discussion has been going on about the
possibility of people who were adopted as babies being
given information about their natural parents, or vice
versa, but it may save great disappointment and frustration if they realise from the beginning that they have
no legal or enforceable rights to such information as the
law stands. However they should talk to the welfare

officer at the Adoption Board who will be able to give the best guidance in these queries.

No civilised person can believe that another human being, however small, can be the 'property' of another, in a way a coat or a book might be, and therefore, the entire community is rightly concerned with the protection of children. People who suspect that a child might be mistreated or neglected at home agonise over what is the best thing to do. Obviously, the worst thing is not to do anything at all about it. If this applies to you, remember that there are agencies to whom you can speak, not only in confidence, but with the assurance that you will not be considered a busybody or troublemaker. The gardai, the social services, the Society for the Prevention of Cruelty to Children are all experienced in being alerted to possibly threatening situations, and will appreciate that you are motivated solely by your concern that a child may be at risk. Sometimes the hesitation arises because of a vague belief that parents have unlimited power to punish their children; they have not, but in any case, that is a judgment that will be made by someone else. The suspicion that a child is helpless and suffering is sufficient grounds to impel us into some action that will enlist the experts. It may be that the only body in the place where you live is the gardai, and if it is not convenient to speak to the officer in charge, you should consider confiding in the local doctor, or a clergyman, someone who knows where help can be speedily got. None of us can remain silent and hope the problem will resolve itself.

I have no doubt that this is one of those situations where it is a great comfort to have a solicitor to whom you can turn. His discretion is assured and his advice will be based on the protection of your own position. He may very well have experience of similar problems before and know what agency is in the best position to help.

THE MOTORIST AND HIS SOLICITOR

12

Besides the buying and selling of houses, the other matter which prompts most people to go to a solicitor on a once-off basis is in connection with a road traffic offence or a motor car accident—quite often, a combination of both. Even a relatively minor prosecution—for exceeding the speed limit somewhat or displaying an out-of-date tax disc—will probably have a motorist consider legal representation, because of the dread possibility of having one's licence endorsed. When prosecuted for a road traffic offence, you are either going to admit it or defend it: if the latter, then you want to put up the best possible defence. It is, after all, the state that is prosecuting you with all its authority and experience; it is quite right to take it very seriously.

The value of a solicitor is that he knows how to present a case. This is not to be confused with silver-tongued oratory. It is simply a matter of knowing the rules of evidence; what is allowed, and what is not. The hearsay rule is the cause of the most difficulty to people conducting their own cases—followed closely by the rule that, in cross-examination, they must ask the witness questions and not start heated arguments with the garda or whoever is giving evidence. Even the most patient judge will eventually weary of assisting an unrepresented party who keeps infringing the rules, because they are too unlike the conventions of ordinary conversation.

It is quite natural to say what someone told you, or to contradict a person who is giving an erroneous account of an event you witnessed. But in court you cannot relate what someone else told you: he must be there to give that evidence himself—which is why gardai, who are accustomed to the procedure, will say things like, 'I saw a man standing outside a blazing house and, as a result of what he said to me, I phoned the Fire Brigade.' Similarly, a lawyer cross-examining a witness will try to have him admit something by a series of questions, but if he fails, he knows he must find another way to prove the point. A skilled questioner can sense if there is a weakness in part of the evidence which could raise a doubt that would lead to a dismissal in his client's favour.

It is universally acknowledged that motorists who cheerfully admit that they cannot sing a note, boil an egg, or draw a straight line, instinctively resent any implication that they are less than perfect drivers. This belief underlies many a civil action, where one motorist is suing another. It can also cause considerable difficulty for a solicitor taking instructions, who will be anxious to ensure that his client is aware of the possibility that a judge may not necessarily share that view. He will want the prospective plaintiff to realise that proving a claim against the other driver will require more than an unshakeable belief in the justice of one's own case. It is not a question of proving that he was blameless, but that the accident was caused solely by the fault of the other driver.

If you are the client, the solicitor will ask about possible witnesses, can they be relied upon to show up and is their evidence likely to be helpful to you? Remember that the court will know nothing about you, the other driver or the

place where the accident happened, except what is
brought out in evidence on the particular day when the
case is heard. If you were fortunate in that only your car
was damaged, not you, the decision may be taken, when
you have had time to digest the information that you will
be first seeking, that it is safer to do the repairs yourself.
You should ask the solicitor about the chances of success,
the extent of the initial costs and outlay, the expert witnesses you will need; and you must also take into account
that, sometimes, no costs are awarded to either side. You
would then stand to lose much more than the actual cost
of repairs, and more still, of course, if you lose and have
to pay the other party's costs.

That is not to say that you should do nothing. Doubtless
your solicitor will already be in correspondence on your
behalf to see what can be gained by negotiation, but the
question will arise as to whether proceedings should be
issued. There is a certain exaggeration in saying, as some
do, that the worst settlement is better than a good fight,
but it does illustrate that people are often led by a natural
desire for vindication rather than by common sense. Bear
with your solicitor when he tries to explain that, at the
end of another year or so, the sense of outrage might have
faded, but that you may be considerably out of pocket.

Other considerations arise where there are personal
injuries or consequential loss, and, in any case, everyone
is entitled to have a case tried in court. If you are told
that a plaintiff has a duty to mitigate his loss, it means
that he must take whatever steps are necessary to mini-
mise the effect of the damage he has suffered. For example,
if my car has been immobilised by the accident, I cannot
abandon it on the side of the road for months on end, and
then complain about the rust. Neither can I claim for
loss of earnings over a long period because I used the car

for my business and did nothing about getting a replacement. I am expected to take the reasonable precautions in my own interest, as I would in any like circumstances.

Kind friends paint rosy pictures of huge compensation awards, urge you to hire the most expensive car and have a glance at the real estate market in Spain. You have every reason to feel that the solicitor is an unimaginative fuddy-duddy by contrast, when he warns you that the legal process is not an exact science. There can be indications, but no certainty, about the amount of the award. You should listen to him on the belt-and-braces principle, and be delighted if the forecast of the friends turns up trumps. You should also hope they will rally around with comfort and support if you lose!

From the time you consult a solicitor about an injury suffered in an accident until the case is heard, two or three years may have passed. A sensible idea is to keep a note of the progress of your recovery in the meantime. It is not to encourage hypochondria, but you obviously will be asked to give evidence about this, and it is impossible readily to recall pain or stiffness in relation to dates. A few lines written in a notebook, every fortnight or so, would be of help.

Ask your solicitor for copies of medical or engineer's reports as he gets them; also, copies of counsel's opinion regarding your case. It is infinitely better that you get the chance to discuss any factual mistake that you spot, at this time, rather than risk contradicting your own witnesses. Apart from that, it familiarises you with the procedure and the evidence, and allows you to contribute your views from the beginning.

SHOPPING AND SERVICES

13

Some time ago, a foreign visitor to Ireland remarked that he was struck by the steady stream of complaints in letters written to the editor of a national newspaper. People complained loud and long about matters he was powerless to remedy, without ever indicating that they had made any representations to those who were responsible for providing the bad service, or no service at all. Not everyone seeks out someone to complain to when things go wrong. Those who do, and are not listened to with patience and courtesy, have genuine cause to feel aggrieved. Many successful plaintiffs will say in court that they were driven to sue because no one was prepared to listen to them or to admit that the slightest blame might attach to management.

If a customer buys an item in which there is a major flaw, she is entitled to have it replaced with a perfect one, and if that is not possible, then to have her money refunded. It is surprising how many people are palmed off with a credit note instead. Sometimes the customer is told it is the fault of the manufacturer. It may well be, but that is a matter between the retailer and the supplier; the only contract the customer made was with the retailer. While the shopkeeper must be given the chance to make good the breach of contract by replacing the unsatisfactory article, nobody should be left out-of-pocket for months on end, being told that the matter is being taken up with the distributors, the importing agency, or that they are awaiting the results of laboratory tests in Japan. That is, of course, if there is no disagreement that the flaw was there at the time of purchase.

A few commercial situations have a sort of built-in urgency about them. With restaurants or taxis, there is no question of anything being supplied on a 'sale or return' basis. Because experience showed that purveyors of meals and transport to the general public were frequently dunned, and the fleeting character of their clientele made the recovery of debt more difficult, it has long been a specific offence not to pay a taxi-driver or restaurant. Under the Debtors (Ireland) Act of 1872, a person who has ordered and eaten a meal in a restaurant for which she cannot pay, may be arrested and charged with obtaining credit on false pretences. A garda has powers, under the Road Traffic Acts, to arrest without a warrant a passenger who has hired a taxi and who has not paid his fare and has refused to give his proper name and address.

So what should you do if you suspect you have been cheated in a restaurant or by a taxi-driver? Keep your receipt and your cool. Where a meal has been unsatisfactory, you make a complaint to the person in charge. You should also let the waiter know during the meal. You are under no obligation to pay for food that you could not eat or that you did not order. In the unlikely event of the proprietor threatening to call the police, remember that the gardai have only power to arrest someone who has no money to pay, not a person who is disputing a bill. You can always pay for that part of the meal which was satisfactory, and leave your name and address. The business of eating out is a matter of simple contract: one party should not be intimidated or embarrassed into accepting a flagrant breach of it by the other.

A solicitor with whom I once worked told me that his grandfather had brought him to Dublin from Kerry for the day when he was ten. They were passing the famous Jammet's Restaurant in Nassau Street. It did not mean anything to the two travellers, except a convenient place to have lunch. The old man waved away the menu and ordered what he considered a simple meal. When the bill came, he was astounded. He felt that there was some mistake; they had never eaten food to that amount. In the middle of the Gallic protestations, the grandfather laid a ten-shilling note on the table and declared that it would amply cover the cost of the meal. He then bent down to retrieve his blackthorn stick, which he had placed under his seat. There fell an instant, wary silence. There was no need for alarm; the old man was a peaceable person, who had never raised his voice in anger, and was not doing so now. He was simply leaving, having settled his just debts. The two walked out of the frozen restaurant, hand-in-hand. It is not to be recommended, of course. The grandfather should have first looked at the bill of fare, but so much fuss is made about de luxe restaurants—it is a story that provides a nice counter-balance!

Taxi passengers are better provided for than any other group of consumers, in the matter of complaints. The Carriage Office at Garda Headquarters in Harcourt Square, Dublin, or the P.S.V. (Public Service Vehicles) Offices at other principal garda stations investigate all complaints with great efficiency and taxi-drivers are regularly prosecuted as a result. Offences range from overcharging for extras, having a dirty cab or failing to pick up a fare at an official stand. If you think you have been overcharged, you should ask for a receipt—and write to the Superintendent in

Charge. It is much more effective than a refusal to pay more than you think fit, which would put you in the wrong from the start.

What has all this got to do with talking to your solicitor? In fact, we have been exploring the ways in which such a necessity can be avoided. For example, the Consumers' Association of Ireland has a scheme to assist people who have complaints about goods or service. It will take the matter up with the retailer, and, if it is a suitable claim, will bring the case to court. The overall fee is quite small and their address is given on page 89 of this book.

There is a Small Claims Court in operation on a pilot basis in Dublin, Swords, Sligo and Cork. It costs only £5 to issue proceedings and there is an official called a Small Claims Registrar at each centre to help any person who wants to enforce a claim, by getting a decree. The court's primary purpose is to make it easier for claimants to do without legal representation, and so save costs. The addresses are given on page 89.·

In spite of all the jokes about buying second-hand cars from the wrong types, it is done all the time, and people get done all the time. We tell each other we know nothing about cars, except how to drive them, but we fail to apply that knowledge, or rather lack of it, when we go to buy one. Obviously, there is protection built into the purchase of a new car, not only as with anything new, but manufacturers are always giving bigger and longer guarantees and warranties, in order to sell them. To buy a second-hand car from a private person is a different matter, not because he has no obligations to us, but because it may be harder to prove the claims that were made about the car's road-worthiness. The seller may prove difficult to pursue; in fact, he may be out of sight within the few weeks it takes the car to fall by the wayside.

It is surprising how many people will buy a car from someone who cannot produce the log book, and then discover that the car was stolen, perhaps even twice in its career! Other unfortunates have sold their car to someone who paid them with a stolen bank draft. A simple phone call to the issuing bank giving the number of the draft could save a lot of grief. A car is a big investment for most of us, who can only afford to buy second-hand cars, and it is not difficult to take some sensible precautions so that we are not taken advantage of. Remember you cannot establish a legal claim to stolen goods, no matter how innocently acquired. The true owner has a prior right to recover his own property, and guilty parties do not hang around long enough to be sued for the recovery of the money you paid them, and for which you are now at a loss. Those few suggestions are quite apart from having a mechanic or motor engineer give the car a thorough examination, which you would be doing in any event. Well, you would, wouldn't you?

If an advertisement has given misleading information, a complaint should be made to the Director of Consumer Affairs, who prosecutes traders if they knowingly or recklessly make untrue statements about service. He also prosecutes persons who engage in fraudulent practices, such as turning back the mileage clock of a car or falsifying its year of manufacture. Sometimes as a result of a successful prosecution, an injured party can get compensation at the same time, but the Director has no role in ordinary commercial transactions. He is a sort of official watchdog on behalf of consumers generally. There is a very good summary of what he does in the Dublin Golden Pages and you can write for further information to his office, whose address is given on page 89. There are several well-produced and helpful information leaflets available there also.

If you do not live in an area where there is a Small Claims Court in operation, or your loss is worth more than £600, you can still issue civil proceedings yourself in the District Court. The forms can be got from legal stationers, and are self-explanatory. If you have difficulty, the staff at the local courthouse will clear up any queries about procedures. However, if you are fairly confident that you have a good case, you should consider a solicitor, because your costs will be recoverable, should you succeed in getting a decree against the trader. Since these are on a scale, or rather on two scales, depending on whether the matter is defended or not, they can be known in advance. Do remember, though, that costs are primarily what we pay our own solicitor. In theory, we recover them, or a portion of them, as being part of the loss we suffered by our opponent's shortcomings. Many solicitors wait for the results of the court hearing, others may require payment in advance.

Not all legal costs are recoverable, apart from those solicitor-and-client fees which cannot be debited to the other side. All these issues should be clarified at the first meeting with the solicitor. You will also take into account the chances of recovering anything from the other party, if you do get a decree against him. This is the most vital question to be faced. It is only when you have all the relevant information, that you can then make the practical decision as to whether it is worth going to court or not. Unfortunately, businesses which are in the habit of giving their customers a bad deal, are frequently those who have several decrees already against them, which they may be paying off by instalments, under court direction. You may decide to throw your hat at it, rather than good money, if you find you will have to wait several years to see any of it come back to you.

TROUBLE WITH THE NEIGHBOURS 14

There must be only very few of us who move into our new home, determined to fight with the neighbours, but it can appear that way to some observers. It is ironical that some of those who are locked into a seemingly endless war with another family in the street, have happy memories of their childhood neighbours. One cannot but wonder what principle is so strong that they feel it is worth depriving their own children of the same kind of nostalgia. It may be that in modern urban conditions people are less dependent on their neighbours for company, help or, indeed, solidarity. They go to work on the other side of town and they can drive to meet close friends on any evening that they do not spend sitting in a curtained room, watching television. Is that why we sometimes boast that we have wonderful neighbours, who never intrude in our lives, but would be there for us if we were ever in any difficulty? In the past, when entertainment and diversion were not instantly to hand, people had the time to form genuine friendships with their neighbours, in a locality where they all spent their free time.

In rural areas, quarrels between neighbours are of more heroic proportions. As Patrick Kavanagh has written, 'I made the Iliad from such a local row.' After all, a few youths kicking a ball in the corner of a big field naturally will not arouse the same ire as if they were doing it in the laneway at the back of suburban houses. So country feuds are seen by the antagonists as being about far graver matters—such as issues to do with land or a slight suffered in a previous generation. Unfortunately, these disputes last longer, perhaps because the families involved are more likely to remain in the same area, and not move house, as they might in a town.

Neighbours quarrel about children, noise, dogs, fences, cars, ball-games, garden refuse. Children feature predominantly in these dramas, usually in combination with one or more of the other causes. Many of the worst effects could be avoided if parents, while listening sympathetically to their children's stories, suspended judgment until they had the opportunity to make their own calm enquiries. Apart from any desire to avoid a row with the neighbours, it is very much in the interest of a child that he be given time and encouragement to admit any fault on his part. It is impossible for him, if he has seen his parents rush down the road on his behalf to have it out with the neighbours, to allow them to lose face by his admitting to any wrongdoing. It will be so much worse, if they also rush to court, to discover that their angel has been in the habit of throwing stones at the neighbour's car or shouting obscenities at the neighbour's wife. Lots of otherwise bright people cannot believe that their own children appear less than perfect to others. Apart from all that, your grandmother would tell you that it is foolish for neighbours to quarrel about their children, because while the parents may not talk for years afterwards, the children will still be playing together the following day! If the matter seems sufficiently serious to consult a solicitor, or make a complaint to the gardai, you should be reasonably satisfied first that you are in possession of all the facts.

The ground can be even more treacherous if the complaint is about a pet, particularly a dog. Some dog owners would rather absorb a thousand insults against their personal honour, than have someone cast aspersions on Bran or Rover. On the other hand, mere common sense tells us that no thinking two-legged creature should be forced into moving house by an irrational four-legged one. A polite but unwavering firmness must be the order of the day, if bins are overturned, ankles are snapped at and no one can sleep because of incessant barking. A person who keeps a dog must accept responsibility for its behaviour. If it is upsetting several households, perhaps two neighbours might call on the owner. If there is no response to this friendly approach, then it becomes obvious that something else must be tried. Unfortunately, once solicitors' letters are dropping onto the neighbour's mat, it will be very difficult for any goodwill to resurface. And that applies equally to a complaint to the local gardai, but this might be more effective, and would certainly be cheaper. It might be worthwhile asking the local residents' association for advice; it must be a matter on which they have considerable experience. You may find that in view of all the new regulations about dogs, residents' groups have evolved some helpful policies or issued leaflets for all dog owners in the locality. It would certainly let everyone know the standard that was expected.

Dividing walls, garden fences and adjoining footpaths have all featured in neighbourly battles, since the beginning of house building. A substantial body of law has developed on the subject of party walls and has added considerably to many a solicitor's practice. A dispute can arise from the roots of a tree in the next garden growing under a wall and coming out the other side. It may foment because of an imaginative use of decoration on top of a plain wall. Others take umbrage because someone else's branches are overhanging their garden. In spite of all the poetry written about trees, it is surprising how much aggression they cause—as do trellises, coping stones, dead leaves and bits of glass on top of walls. There is a lot to be said for concreting every patch of earth.

Those who have done everything in their power to preserve peace and goodwill cannot be expected to sacrifice the enjoyment of their own property indefinitely. If the friendly approach and the reasonable request has not worked, you are certainly justified in going to a solicitor. You will have little choice if the dispute is about a boundary. It will save time if you can bring a map with you, showing the location of your house and garden, and, if possible, a copy of your title. The solicitor can get a copy with your permission but it is a pity that few solicitors think of giving their clients a photo-copy of their main title deed, when they buy a house, before the original disappears into the vaults of the banks and building societies forever. A fee is usually payable just to look at them again. If it is a matter of damage to your property, bring photographs with you, or anything else that will help you to explain the background as clearly as possible the first time.

Complaints about noise, unpleasant smells or fumes should be made to the Environmental Health Officer in the area. There are regulations governing noise pollution, including loud music. It is possible for a few people to take out a summons in the District Court giving seven days' notice to a resident in the neighbourhood to abate a nuisance, such as a barking dog, otherwise he or she is liable to a penalty. It is expected that there will soon be specific regulations setting a time limit on the ringing of burglar alarms and other inconsiderate behaviour. Planning laws are there for the benefit of the entire community, and no one should be allowed to get away with a monstrous breach of them simply because he or she is a decent person, or we do not want to have any argument. In the end, it only leads to resentment, because it is a kind of emotional bullying when the offender relies on the neighbours not speaking out from timidity. Provided that you are determined not to have a row about it, you certainly should make your views known very firmly. If the other person chooses never to speak to you again as a punishment, you really are not going to miss the conversation very much.

Because there is strength in numbers, the most practical help in neighbourhood problems will be found in the local residents' associations. They have developed, by experience over the years, the facility of dealing with local and central government on a variety of issues. Many of them have a solicitor on their committee, or one with which they consult regularly when the need arises. It is well worthwhile seeking out a member, or going to a meeting to voice your concern or to get advice. The central body is called ACRA and its address is given on page 92. You can obtain the address of the one in your own locality from there, if needs be.

This brief look at possible ways in which a dispute between neighbours might be resolved, short of legal action, is useful because, if you do consult a solicitor, he is likely to mention them to you. Prospective clients are often irritated by what they see as a lawyer's reluctance to take decisive action, without delay or equivocation. Because they are cross or upset, they cannot appreciate that it will be more profitable, financially and socially, to see first if negotiation has a chance.

You would have every right to feel aggrieved if a solicitor allowed you to embark upon an action without making you aware of the possible pitfalls. Take a perennial cause of rows, the maintenance of common boundaries, from chimney stacks in towns to hedges in the country. An example of this is if my neighbour has not reimbursed me for the cost of the repairs which were agreed between us. I am very angry because, not only is it a breach of faith, but I had no choice but to have the work done, in order to avoid more serious damage. It is unjust that he should be allowed to get away with this; in my present mood I do not care what it will cost me to force him to this recognition. Through talking to a solicitor, I may accept that the few hundred pounds that is at stake is not worth the possible loss of a thousand or more later on. I could also emerge armed with advice on what to do in any similar situation, which may in the long run be worth the experience for the lesson that has been learnt.

COMPLAINTS ABOUT A SOLICITOR

In this final chapter, we shall consider the situation where you have serious misgivings about your solicitor, either about the service you are receiving or his failure to deal with your affairs in line with your instructions. Long delays in pursuing a matter and the feeble excuses which follow make clients despair; they feel frustrated and helpless. They see no progress being made, and the problem, which they had hoped would be lifted from their shoulders, seems weightier than ever.

If any one of the above applies to you, then it must be realised, first and foremost, that there is no reason why this state of affairs should continue; decide that you are going to do something about it—today. You may not want, at this stage, to make a formal complaint—we shall come to that procedure shortly—because it may delay matters further. A practical step would be to make a firm appointment for a date about two weeks later, and, having done that, follow it up immediately with a letter listing the questions that you want to discuss at the meeting and which you are sure he will be able to clarify. If a specific instruction was not followed, then you expect that he has persuasive reasons for not doing so, which he will be telling you about when you meet. Your letter will alert him to the fact that you are aware no real progress has been made, and that you are giving him a reasonable, but limited, time to do something about it.

After the meeting you might write again confirming the points that were raised, what course is going to be followed and when you will expect to hear from him, as soon as the proceedings have been served or the contract has been sent out, or whatever is appropriate. All these exchanges can be conducted with politeness, but not with any great warmth. After all, it is he who should be showing the goodwill, not you. Keep photocopies of your letters, so that you have a record. This all may seem game-playing, and what you really want to do is to go and tell him what you think of him, and storm out with your file of papers. It could very well be the better course, if it is in the early stages, or if nothing has been done at all. However, there may have been a process which has advanced to a point and then stopped. It might need to be started again from the beginning with a new solicitor—like negotiations, perhaps. You may consider that it is worth one more effort with the old firm. In either case, you are not burning any bridges, and this is one time when you should consider nobody's interest but your own. If there has been no progress discernible within five weeks—or sooner, if the matter is urgent—then you should make a formal complaint.

If you telephone the Incorporated Law Society, whose address and telephone number are given on page 88, and speak to an official there, she or he will advise you how to proceed, or you could write or call in. Put together in a file any correspondence that you have so that you can refresh your memory about dates and instructions. The Society will write to the solicitor telling him of your complaint and asking for his views. It can be enough to get things moving satisfactorily again.

There are changes planned in the way in which complaints will in the future be handled by the Society under the Solicitors (Amendment) Bill 1991, which at the time of writing has only just come before the Dáil for consideration. It is a very comprehensive piece of legislation, but, briefly, it will empower the Society to investigate a complaint and direct the particular solicitor to rectify errors and omissions, to refund costs or to transfer documents to another solicitor, among other remedies. There is provision for lay members to be part of a disciplinary committee to whom complaints about solicitors' misconduct will be referred, and an independent adjudicator to deal with complaints by members of the public about the way their original complaint was handled by the Society.

All this is in the future and there may be many changes before the Act finally becomes law. In the meantime, a useful thing to remember is that solicitors are accustomed to confrontation with each other; it forms the basis of a lot of their working day. You should not jump to the conclusion that it is useless to make a complaint about one solicitor to another; they have not got the same perceived solidarity as other professions. Naturally, this applies to a bigger town rather than to a smaller, because of the numbers practising in any one place. However, you are not confined to going to a local solicitor to ask him to write to the one that is giving you all the heartache. While it seems unreasonable to be paying two solicitors for the same work, it may be worth some expenditure in the hope of getting a quicker response. It is not at all unusual for a client, who is having trouble with one solicitor, to go and talk to another about it.

Nevertheless, you may be reluctant to consider such a step because it appears to place you in the double jeopardy of the second solicitor proving as dilatory as the first.

The most direct way then is a straightforward complaint to his professional body and you should pursue it vigorously with the Society. It is important that the matter should not be allowed to drag on without resolution since this will lead to frustration piled upon the anxiety you have already experienced. People go to solicitors in the first place for information and reassurance and it is a shame if they are left in a worse muddle than before. The truth is that some clients give up at that stage but the problem is not solved. It will resurface at some time in the future and will be all the more difficult to untangle. It is little comfort to have avoided some initial unpleasantness if you are going to have to explain your own inertia to another party later.

Of course it is far better not to allow the relationship with our solicitor to come to this sad end. We would be much better tackling the inefficiency or misunderstandings when they happen, rather than let them accumulate. When a letter is not replied to or a telephone call unreturned, there is no reason why excuses about pressure of work should be accepted. Some people talk about 'being busy' as if it were a rare tropical infection which they alone suffer from. Everyone of us is busy about our own affairs and what are solicitors' affairs but their clients'? So that we do not want to hear from those who are providing a service that other people are somehow more important than we are. Do remember that there are hundreds of good solicitors to whom every client is a special individual, and there is no reason to prevent you establishing an enduring connection with one of them, from which you will both learn a great deal.

ADDRESSES OF USEFUL SERVICES

General Advice

The Incorporated Law Society of Ireland,
Blackhall Place,
Dublin 7.   (01) 710711

Office of the Ombudsman,
52, St Stephen's Green,
Dublin 2.   (01) 785222

Legal Aid Board,
47, Upper Mount Street,
Dublin 2.   (01) 615811

The Board has Law Centres in Dublin, Cork, Dundalk,
Letterkenny, Sligo, Athlone and Galway.
The addresses can be found in the Telephone Directory
for each place.

FLAC (Free Legal Advice Centre),
49, South William Street,
Dublin 2.   (01) 6794239

FLAC will particularly give advice in employment and
Social Welfare claims.

National Social Service Board,
71, Lower Leeson Street,
Dublin 2.   (01) 616422

The Board has set up Citizens' Information Centres throughout the country. Their addresses and opening hours will be found in the Yellow Pages.

Consumer Rights

Consumers' Association of Ireland,
45, Upper Mount Street,
Dublin 2.   (01) 612466

Small Claims Registrar,
Aras Ui Dalaigh,
Four Courts,
Dublin 7.   (01) 725555
                                             ext. 127

also at: District Court Office, Sligo.
            District Court Office, Cork.
            District Court Office, Swords, Co. Dublin.

Director of Consumer Affairs and Fair Trade,
4th Floor, Shelbourne House,
Shelbourne Road,
Dublin 4.   (01) 613399

Marriage and Family

There is a Registrar of Marriages for every county. The local Health Board will have details of the nearest official, or you may write direct to the Registrar in Dublin:

Mr R.V.H. Downey,
31, Molesworth Street,
Dublin 2.   (01) 767485/763218/9

Marriage Counselling Service,
24, Grafton Street,
Dublin 2.   (01) 720341

Catholic Marriage Advisory Council,
All Hallows College,
Drumcondra,
Dublin 9.   (01) 375649
Consult telephone directory for local centres.

AIM Group for Family Law Reform,
64, Lower Mount Street,
Dublin 2.   (01) 616478

Family Mediation Service,
Block 1, 5th Floor,
Irish Life Centre,
Lower Abbey Street,
Dublin 1.   (01) 728277

Clanwilliam Institute,
18, Clanwilliam Terrace,
Grand Canal Quay,
Dublin 2.   (01) 761363

Children

Child Care Officers attached to the regional Health
Boards, of which there are eight:
Eastern: Dublin, Kildare, Wicklow
Midland: Laois, Longford, Offaly, Westmeath
Mid Western: Clare, Limerick, Tipperary North Riding
South Eastern: Carlow, Kilkenny, Tipperary South
Riding, Waterford, Wexford

North Eastern: Cavan, Louth, Meath, Monaghan
North Western: Donegal, Leitrim, Sligo
Southern: Cork, Kerry
Western: Galway, Mayo, Roscommon

Federation of Services for Unmarried Parents and their
Children,
36, Upper Rathmines Road,
Rathmines,
Dublin 6.   (01) 964155

This organisation provides an information and referral
service on a national basis. They have a wide range of
informational leaflets on related matters.

Welfare Officer,
Adoption Board (An Bord Uchtala),
Hawkins House,
Dublin 2.   (01) 715888

Adoption Advice Service,
Barnardo's,
244, Harolds Cross Road,
Dublin 6.   (01) 960042
Every Tuesday, 14.00–18.00

Irish Society for the Prevention of Cruelty to Children,
20, Molesworth Street,
Dublin 2.   (01) 6794944
Freephone   (1800) 666666

Childline Advisory Service   (01) 793333
Consult also local directory.

Neighbourhood

ACRA, Central Body for Residents' Associations,
30, Newtown Drive,
Ayrfield,
Dublin 13.   (01) 8470224

Environmental Health Officer and Housing Officer of
the Local Authority in the area.

For up-to-date information on regulations made under
planning and Housing Acts:

Press and Information Officer,
Department of the Environment,
Custom House,
Dublin 1.   (01) 6793377

Death

The Registrar,
Probate Office,
Four Courts,
Dublin 7.   (01) 725555

District Probate Registries: contact the County
Registrar in the principal county town.

For information on organ donation:
Irish Kidney Association,
Donor House,
156, Pembroke Road,
Dublin 4.   (01) 689788/9

Civil Liberties

Irish Association of Civil Liberty,
8, Dawson Street,
Dublin 2.

Irish Council for Civil Liberties,
36, The Rise,
Boden Park,
Rathfarnham,
Dublin 16.   (01) 944575

Garda Siochana Complaints Board,
Block 1, 5th Floor,
Irish Life Centre,
Lower Abbey Street,
Dublin 1.   (01) 728666

The Superintendent,
Carriage Office,
Garda Headquarters,
Harcourt Square,
Dublin 2.   (01) 732222

GLOSSARY

Important. The definitions given below are not exhaustive. They are simple explanations of the meaning of the words as they are used in the text.

to affirm   to give a solemn promise, without a religious basis, to tell the truth in court

barring order   a decree of a court that a spouse leave the family home and remain away for a stated period

beneficiary   a person who receives a benefit under a will

bequest   a gift left by will, also called a legacy

breach of contract   occurs where a condition of a legally-binding agreement has been broken

brief   a statement of a case written out for a barrister together with copies of relevant documents, also used as slang term for a lawyer

burden of proof   onus of proving a case, which in criminal matters must be discharged by the prosecutor beyond reasonable doubt; in civil proceedings the plaintiff must prove the case on the balance of probabilities

caveat   official notice of intention to contest a will

conveyancing   the process by which ownership of land and building is transferred *counsel* alternative word for barrister, singular or plural

damages compensation awarded for injury to person or property

encumbrances prior right over land belonging to persons other than the owner, such as mortgage, rent, rights-of-way

endorsement details of convictions for driving offences noted officially on a person's licence

estreatment bail money forfeited to the State because the accused did not observe the terms under which bail was granted

executor a person named in a will to carry out directions given

grant of probate the record under which the assets of a deceased person are officially distributed

joint-ownership where property is equally owned by more than one person and passes to the survivor on death, for example houses or bank accounts

log-book the form issued by a local authority to a motorist showing technical details of a car such as make, year, size and previous owners

negligence failure of a legal duty to take proper care

party walls any common boundary to adjoining properties

pre-nuptial before a marriage

protection order a court direction that one spouse is not to threaten or molest the other; the party who disobeys can be arrested without warrant

residuary estate property remaining after specific gifts given by a will are accounted for

testamentary freedom   a right to leave our property in whatever manner we please

title a person's right to own a specific property, and also the written record of it in a deed

undertaking a binding promise made by a solicitor on behalf of his client, usually to pay out money coming in or to hand over title deeds to a bank or building society

INDEX